The Case for Free Trade and Open Immigration

Edited by
Richard M. Ebeling
and
Jacob G. Hornberger

THE FUTURE
OF FREEDOM
FOUNDATION

Fairfax, Virginia

ISBN 0-9640447-4-9 — ISBN 0-9640447-3-0 (pbk.)
Copyright © 1995

Permission is granted to reprint, copy, and redistribute any item in
this book without special permission except "The United States: A
Protectionist Nation" and "The Immorality of Protectionism" by James
Bovard, "Value Added" by Ron K. Unz, "Foreign Policy" by Bettina Bien
Greaves, and "The Freedom to Move as an International Problem" by
Ludwig von Mises. Please send two copies of reprints to The Foundation.

The Future of Freedom Foundation
11350 Random Hills Road
Suite 800
Fairfax, Virginia 22030

Library of Congress
Catalog Card Number: 94-061115

Published 1995
Printed in the United States of America

Contents

Founded in 1989, The Future of Freedom Foundation is a tax-exempt, educational foundation that presents an uncompromising moral, philosophical, and economic case for individual freedom, private property, and limited government. The Foundation aims to influence a shift in thinking away from the welfare-state, managed-economy philosophy toward the private-property, free-market philosophy.

Most of the essays in this volume appeared in the monthly publication of The Foundation, Freedom Daily. *Subscribers come from thirty countries. The price for a one-year subscription to* Freedom Daily *is $15 ($20 foreign).*

Preface

Throughout history, people have permitted their government officials to regulate and control their peaceful activities. The age-old idea is that government "owns" its citizens and, therefore, has the power to manage their behavior.

The American Revolution in 1776 overthrew that bankrupt notion. For the first time in history, a citizenry openly proclaimed that their lives, their liberties, and their properties were rights endowed in them by the Creator, not by government. Government officials, the American people said, were simply servants whose job was to protect, not regulate or destroy, these God-given rights.

The result was the most unusual society in history. Throughout most of the period from 1787 to the 1900s, there was no income taxation, welfare, Social Security, public schooling, war on poverty, or war on drugs. And except for certain tariffs that were unfortunately imposed, people were free to travel and trade anywhere in the United States and in the world without the interference of U.S. government officials. With the tragic exception of American slaves, the American people were the freest people in history.

And the result? The result was the most economically prosperous nation in the history of man. And the healthiest. And the most literate. And the most charitable.

And all this occurred despite the fact that thousands of penniless immigrants, many of whom could not speak English, were flooding American shores every day—escaping the lands of government control to come to the land of freedom. Americans had let the word go forth all over the world: "If you can escape the political dungeons or the economic misery in your own countries, there is a place you can come."

Unfortunately, twentieth-century Americans have abandoned the principles of freedom of their ancestors. They have restored government as the sovereign power over their lives. The U.S. today has the same governmental controls and interventions as those in all other nations: income taxation, welfare, Social Security, economic regulations, public schooling, trade restrictions, and immigration controls. The results have been: reduced standards of living, increased dependency on governmental largess, and high rates of illiteracy. And, of course, the Statue of Liberty now stands as a cruel mockery to people who are suffering and dying all over the world and who have no place to go.

Individuals have the God-given right to live their lives the way they choose, so long as they do not inflict violence or fraud on others. They have the right to enter into mutually beneficial exchanges with others anywhere in the world. They have the right to keep the fruits of their earnings. They have the right to dispose of their money the way they want. They have the right to travel and move without political restriction. It is the duty of government to protect, not regulate or destroy, these inherent, fundamental rights.

It is time to repeal, not reform, America's welfare-state, regulated-economy way of life. It is time to repeal all trade restrictions and immigration controls. It is time to recapture the principles and spirit of liberty on which our nation was founded. Our peace and well-being depend on it.

—Jacob G. Hornberger
Founder and President
The Future of Freedom Foundation

Introduction

Have you ever thought about what a free world would look like? What a world would look like in which men were free to trade with whomever they wanted and wherever they wanted? What a world would look like in which men could travel and live wherever they found it most advantageous and pleasurable? What a world would look like in which anyone could spend their money or invest their savings in any part of the globe in which it seemed most profitable and beneficial to them? A world in which there were neither immigration restrictions nor emigration barriers? A world in which goods could move freely from one country to another with neither tariffs nor quotas on the amounts that could enter or exit a country? A world in which individuals could trade and contract in any form of money they found most profitable, with neither currency nor financial constraints?

Almost none of us presently alive have ever known such a world, but it did exist once, and not that long ago. Indeed, it was the type of world that encompassed a sizable part of the globe before the First World War. A picture of it was given by the famous English economist John Maynard Keynes in his book *The Economic Consequences of the Peace* (1919):

> What an extraordinary episode in the economic progress of man that age was which came to an end in August, 1914! The greater part of the population, it is true, worked hard and lived at a low standard of comfort, yet, were, to all appearances, reasonably contented with this lot. But escape was possible, for any man of capacity or character at all exceeding the average, into the middle and upper classes, for whom life offered, at a low cost and with the least trouble, conveniences, comforts, and amenities beyond the compass of the richest and most powerful monarchs of other ages. The inhabitant of London could order

by telephone, sipping his morning tea in bed, the various products of the whole earth, in such quantity as he might see fit, and reasonably expect their early delivery upon his doorstep; he could at the same moment and by the same means adventure his wealth in the natural resources and new enterprises of any quarter of the world, and share, without exertion or even trouble, in their prospective fruits and advantages; or he could decide to couple the security of his fortunes with the good faith of the townspeople of any substantial municipality in any continent that fancy or information might recommend. He could secure, forthwith, if he wished it, cheap and comfortable means of transit to any country or climate without passport or other formality, could despatch his servant to the neighboring office of a bank for such supply of the precious metals as might seem convenient, and could then proceed abroad to foreign quarters, without knowledge of their religion, language, or customs, bearing coined wealth upon his person, and would consider himself greatly aggrieved and much surprised at the least interference. But most important of all, he regarded this state of affairs as normal, certain, and permanent, except in the direction of further improvement, and any deviation from it as aberrant, scandalous, and avoidable. The projects and politics of militarism and imperialism, of racial and cultural rivalries, of monopolies, restrictions, and exclusion, which were to play the serpent to this paradise, were little more than the amusements of his daily newspaper, and appeared to exercise almost no influence at all on the ordinary course of social and economic life, the internationalization of which was nearly complete in practice.

This world was the achievement of the 19th-century classical liberals. Beginning in the 18th century, with such notable spokesmen as David Hume and Adam Smith, the classical liberals argued that both liberty and prosperity could be more readily attained if the state withdrew from practically all intervention in the market and left the course of economic activity to the free choices of private individuals. The lure of profits by satisfying consumer demand and the pressure of peaceful competition among rivals in the market would assure that the self-interested behavior of each participant in the market would be directed to serve the interests of others in the society. The early classical liberals advocated what Adam Smith called "a system of natural liberty," in which the state would be limited to a handful of functions, primarily the protection of life and property from domestic violence, national defense against foreign aggression, and the adjudication of disputes and the enforcement of contracts through a system of courts under the rule of law.

Beyond this, the classical liberals sometimes argued with each other over whether there were some other duties for the state to perform. But their basic premise was that practically all other matters were best left to the voluntary efforts of the free individuals of the society. If a proposal was made for the state to undertake more than these limited tasks, the burden of proof was upon the advocate of intervention to demonstrate that some shortcoming in the natural working of the market economy and any government regulation or interference would not, in fact, make worse the particular problem the intervener hoped to cure through the use of state power.

From the middle decades of the 19th century until the beginning of the First World War in 1914, most of the countries of Europe and North America predominantly followed the path of economic liberty. And, in practice, economic liberty meant a mostly unregulated market at home and free trade and free immigration in international affairs. While far from being a perfect world, never had the world been more depoliticized. While wars still occasionally occurred, and while politics still sometimes crept into economic relationships among the citizens of different countries, these occurrences were limited and minimized precisely because it was not the duty of the state to concern itself with the outcomes of the market, but merely to enforce the legal "rules of the game" under which individuals peacefully traded and freely exchanged with one another.

With most of the countries of Europe and North America following the same classical-liberal rules of the game, the world, for the most part, became a cosmopolitan market and civil society. Nationalist prejudices, rivalries, and conflicts were restrained and, to a great extent, eliminated. The market was the entire globe, and one's trading partners and potential customers were all the other citizens of this free-trade world.

The free market tends to be both color-blind and nationality-blind. It treats all participants equally. As a customer, the market only asks, is the individual offering the best price to the seller? As a producer, the market only asks, is the individual offering the best price to the buyer? The market ignores where the buyer or seller comes from, what language he speaks, or what religion he professes; it binds all participants into one interconnected network of division of labor and mutual benefit through voluntary exchange.

Political power, violent conflict, and national passions are replaced with voluntary interdependency, peaceful competition, and international tranquillity.

How different our own times are from those before 1914. Today, politics intrudes into everything. Both domestic commerce and international trade are regulated and controlled by the state. We live not in the era of liberty but in the age of politics. What does this mean? English historian Ronald M. Hartwell helps us to understand:

> Politicization can be defined as that now pervasive tendency for making all questions political questions, all issues political issues, all values political values, and all decisions political decisions. . . . Politicization thus takes the manifest form of increasing the power of the state, of increasing political power as against all other forms of power in society, of increasing the power of the politicians and the bureaucrats as against the power of individuals, private institutions, and voluntary associations. . . . Today the individual . . . is constantly aware of the state, over which he can exercise little or no control even though it makes more and more decisions about his life.

Today, international trade is no longer the cumulative pattern of private exchanges among a multitude of buyers and sellers, who by accident of birth or conscious choice just happen to reside in different countries of the world. No, today all international transactions are matters of politics and national interest as defined by those who at a moment in time hold high political office and speak for the collection of special interests who have brought them to power in the last election. Shall a particular commodity be allowed into the country? Will a specific raw material be permitted to enter the nation? At what financial penalty—at what rate of tariff—shall the citizens of a country be allowed to purchase the goods offered for sale from another nation? National politics now determine these things, rather than private individuals peacefully pursuing profit to better their own lives.

But what about the international organizations established by the governments of the world—the General Agreement on Tariffs and Trade (GATT), the World Bank, the International Monetary Fund (IMF), the International Labor Organization (ILO), and numerous others—to facilitate the lowering of trade barriers and creation of an international order of freer trade? The establishment of free trade is a simple process for any government to introduce. From a specified date, all barriers and restrictions on the free movement and exchange of goods and services, raw materials and resources, and the free movement of all peoples are abolished. The exchange of goods and the movement of commodities and people from that day forth are free from governmental control and regulation and, thus, are depoliticized. This is all governments need to do and should do. And it can be done in short order through the passage and signing of legislation repealing all political prohibitions on the freedom of trade and the freedom of movement.

But this is not the purpose of the international organizations established by the governments of the world. Their purpose is to facilitate *politically managed trade.* Governments use these organizations and international forums to control and plan the terms under which goods may be sold to each other on the world market and the conditions under which resources and commodities may enter each other's countries. Towards the end of the Second World War, when many of these international organizations were being established, free-market economist Henry Hazlitt analyzed the nature of the problem in an article entitled "Free Trade or State Domination?" in *The American Scholar* (Winter, 1944-45):

> For government officials, even when they really understand (which is very rarely) the basic economic forces that they are trying to control, are almost never disinterested. They are almost certain to reflect the special interests of some political pressure group. The interests of the pressure groups represented by the bureaucrats of one nation are certain to clash with those of the pressure groups represented by the bureaucrats of another. And these conflicting interests, precisely because they are represented by their respective governments, are far more likely to clash openly, directly and politically than in a world of genuine free trade. . . . [W]hat the planners mean by free trade [is] . . . not the freedom of ordinary people to buy and sell, lend and borrow, at whatever prices and rates they like and wherever they find it most profitable to do so. . . . They mean . . . the freedom of bureaucrats to settle these matters for [them].

This has been the reality of the structure and patterns of international trade since the end of World War II, when these international institutions came into existence.

But nowhere has the heavy hand of state control over international affairs in our century been so harmful and cruel as in the arena of human migration. Since the First World War, governments throughout the world have introduced or reinforced the barriers to the free movement of people from one part of the world to another. People in poverty or political fear in their home countries have been unable to escape—or severely restrained in their ability to escape—from their poor or oppressive conditions. It has been bad enough that often the governments under which they have lived, viewing them as the "property" of the state, have prevented or restricted their ability to escape to a freer land. But it has been the blackest mark on the conscience of those freer countries to deny entry to many, if not most, of these wandering souls when they have been lucky enough to find ways to exit from their countries of origin.

In the 1970s, thousands of Vietnamese fled their homeland to escape from communist tyranny; many still languish in refugee camps in various parts of southeast Asia. Chinese escaping from their communist homeland have drowned in the waves off America's shores as they have tried to avoid arrest by the Coast Guard and the agents of the Immigration and Naturalization Service. In 1993 and 1994, our television screens were filled with images of boatloads of Haitians escaping from political tyranny and economic poverty; they have been either forced back to their fate in Haiti or have faced an uncertain future in holding areas policed by the U. S. military. Member states of the European Union have instituted new, more stringent rules and bureaucratic procedures to weed out those who are asking for immigrant or refugee status in Western Europe from Eastern Europe, North Africa, or the Middle East, with many of these unfortunate human beings running away from the violence in the former Yugoslavia or the repression and terrorism of Moslem fundamentalists in Algeria. At the very time that means and costs of transportation from one part of the globe to another have become increasingly accessible and affordable for a growing number of people, governments have attempted to raise the political drawbridge to prevent people from living and traveling to where they desire.

All such practices succeed in doing is either forcing many of these potential immigrants to continue to languish in poverty and repression in their home countries or living lives as illegals in a politically hostile host country. Periodically the press will run stories on the hardships and exploitation that many of these illegal immigrants suffer, e.g., in the United States. The newspapers will point out that they work for below-market wages because their illegal employers threaten them with exposure and deportation if they "cause trouble" and ask for a higher salary or commonly received fringe benefits. The fact that they come to and work in America even under these lower-than-market conditions means that the employment they find still represents an opportunity to earn money for themselves and their families that is better than in their home country. But their hardships and employment disadvantage are precisely due to their illegal status. If they could enter the country openly and legally, no employer could long retain them for wages and benefits less than those offered to workers of equal skill employed elsewhere in the American economy; if some employers tried to do so, these new members in the American workforce would "migrate" to better jobs in other sectors of the market. Thus, government immigration restrictions actually assist the exploitation of these new—albeit illegal—Americans.

It is time to move beyond the age of politics and to advance to a new and even freer and more prosperous era of liberty. Freedom of trade and freedom of movement are two of the essential hallmarks of a society of free men. If a human being is denied the right and opportunity to earn his livelihood how and where he finds it most advantageous and agreeable, then in the most fundamental sense he is not a free man but a tool of those who control the governments of the world. He is a puppet whose very movement is determined and controlled by another. Are we not tired of political control and economic manipulation by the state after all the disastrous consequences of big government in our century? Is it not time to say to every human being: Work at what you want, trade with whomever you desire, live wherever you feel happiest.

The Future of Freedom Foundation exists to bring the United States and the world closer to that new era of liberty in which every man will be free to do these things. The essays in this volume make the case for complete free trade and unrestricted free immigration. The majority of them have appeared in previous issues of the Foundation's monthly publication, *Freedom Daily.* Some are reprinted from other publications, with the hope that together they present the most consistent case for global freedom. If we succeed in this fight, the 21st century may, indeed, be the noblest and most majestic in human history.

—*Richard M. Ebeling*
Vice President of Academic Affairs
The Future of Freedom Foundation

1

The Case for Unilateral Free Trade and Open Immigration

by Jacob G. Hornberger

The American people are extremely fortunate. Two hundred years ago, their Founding Fathers used the Constitution to prohibit American government officials from ever enacting trade and immigration restrictions between the respective states of the Union. This meant that the citizens of any state could buy and sell goods and services with the citizens of any other state, without tariffs or import restrictions. It also meant that citizens of one state could travel or move to another state without permission, passport, or other restriction.

Most American politicians and bureaucrats today honestly believe that free trade and open immigration are harmful to a society. Therefore, if today's government officials were not prohibited by the Constitution from enacting trade and immigration controls between the respective states, life in the United States would be dramatically different. Each state would enact a host of import restrictions, tariffs, and immigration controls to protect the citizenry from "foreigners" and "foreign goods" from other parts of the country.

For example, the state of Georgia would impose import quotas on goods from Florida. Why? Because there is a trade imbalance between the two states—that is, Georgians are purchasing more from

1

Floridians than Floridians are purchasing from Georgians. There would be trade negotiations and trade summits between the governors of the two states, as they tried to negotiate the trade imbalance between their respective states. If the negotiations failed, a trade war between Georgia and Florida would ensue.

Another example, the state of Texas would impose strict immigration controls restricting the immigration into Texas of those weird New Yorkers. After all, there is a high unemployment rate in Texas and, therefore, the Texas economy could not absorb an additional inflow of people. Moreover, an influx of New Yorkers would cause wages in Texas to drop—and the New Yorkers emigrating to Texas would take jobs away from Texans.

Kansas would impose immigration controls on California, because the latter has a much higher incidence of AIDS cases. "We can't permit free immigration from California," the Kansas officials would say, "because we might get inundated by AIDS patients.

Fortunately, due to the wisdom and foresight of Americans two hundred years ago, these types of restrictions cannot be imposed by American politicians and bureaucrats today. And make no mistake about it—the *only* reason they are not imposed is because the Constitution does now allow their imposition. Without these constitutional restrictions, American politicians and bureaucrats, being firmly committed to the idea of trade and immigration controls—and being so subject to the pressures, influences, and financial contributions of special-interest groups—and believing that trade and immigration restrictions are the key to economic prosperity—would riddle American society with them.

It is impossible to overstate the importance and benefits Americans have in living in what is the largest free-trade and free-immigration zone in the world. We travel across state boundaries and never see a customs or immigration official. In fact, the usual way we know we are in a different state is that we see a road sign that says: "Welcome to the state of. . . ." We buy and sell goods across state lines without ever concerning ourselves with whether we are violating some type of tariff or import or export control—or with whether we are alleviating or aggravating some trade imbalance with another state.

And it is this principle—the principle of free trade and open immigration within the fifty states—that is one of the major reasons that the American people have—and have had—the highest standard of living in history.

For standards of living of people can rise through the mere act of exchange!

2

For example, suppose you have ten oranges and I have ten apples. I value one of your oranges more than my tenth apple; and you value one of my apples more than your tenth orange. We trade—one apple for one orange. Our standard of living has improved—through the mere act of exchange! Thus, the more people are free to trade, the higher the standards of living tend to be.

And the same principle applies internationally—when people are free to trade and travel—whether it is with people of another state, another city, or another nation—they are able to improve their standards of living.

Then, why have American government officials (despite their apparent devotion to freedom) imposed a strangulating set of import restrictions and tariffs on the goods and services coming into the U.S.? And why have they tightly restricted the flow of people traveling or moving to the U.S.?

The reason lies in politics and special-interest groups.

Consider the following example. Suppose a Toyota is priced at $15,000. A Chevrolet Impala, let us say, sells for the same price. You, as a consumer, decide that you like the quality of the Toyota better. You decide to buy the Toyota.

General Motors screams to the U.S. government: "Force Mary to buy from General Motors." Union workers chime in: "Mary's purchase of a Toyota will take our jobs away." Government officials bow under the pressure. They do not force Mary to buy the Impala. But they say to Mary: "If you buy the Toyota, you pay $15,000 to Toyota and a $5,000 tariff (tax) to the U.S. government." If Mary buys the Chevrolet, her standard of living—from her perspective—is not as high as it could have been. If she buys the Toyota, the government has, in effect, legally stolen the sum of $5,000 from her; and her standard of living has dropped by $5,000.

The worst part of it is that the people who pay the biggest price for tariffs and import restrictions are the poor, because these taxes are regressive—that is, their weight falls disproportionately greater on poor people. In other words, the same government that professes to have such a big concern for the poor with its welfare state, impoverishes the poor through trade restrictions for the sake of wealthy special-interest groups.

Consider immigration controls. There are good and honorable people from the Republic of Mexico today sitting in American penitentiaries along the Mexican border. Their crime? Trying to enter into a trade with an American—a trade by which both of their standards of living would be improved. The Mexican wants to work, and an American wants to hire him. But the same government that

3

"loves" the poor with its welfare state, slams the jailhouse door on the poor who have committed the heinous American crime of trying to improve their lives through labor.

Consider the Haitian people. Using its political and military power to control international trade, the U.S. government has imposed a trade embargo on the Haitian people—using force to prevent goods and services from reaching Haiti, which, in turn, has caused death and destitution from starvation. Then, when the Haitian people attempt to survive by trying to escape to the U.S., American government officials capture them and forcibly return them to the death and destitution that awaits them. In other words, despite its supposed devotion to the poor through the welfare state, the U.S. government, through its powers over trade and immigration, condemns thousands of the poorest people in the world to death and destitution.

The ultimate argument against trade and immigration controls, however, lies not in economic terms—that is, that free trade and open immigration result in higher standards of living. The real argument lies in moral principles. A person has the right to do what he wants with his own money. He has a right to buy anything he wishes from whoever wishes to sell to him. He has a right to sell what belongs to him to whoever wishes to buy it. He has a right to employ anyone he wishes, so long as the employee wants to work there. He has a right to work for anyone, so long as the employer wants him to work there. Individuals have a right to travel and trade—whether domestically or internationally—without interference from government officials.

What should be the trade and immigration policy of the United States—and, for that matter, all other nations? To unilaterally drop—without negotiations, agreements, or treaties—all trade and immigration controls. This would mean that Americans, upon returning from an overseas trip, would return to the U.S. in the same way they return to Dallas from San Francisco—without ever waiting in a line to see a customs or immigration official. It would also mean that people all over the world could simply get on a plane and travel to Minneapolis or New York or Memphis, also without ever having to see a customs or immigration official. It would mean that businessmen all over the world could buy from Americans and sell to Americans the same way that Texans buy from and sell to Virginians.

What is the response of the "controllers" to a world of free trade and open immigration?

"They'll go on welfare." Well, one solution is to end the dole for everyone, including Americans. Alternatively, immigrants are not citizens; therefore, there is no requirement that they be permitted to be on the dole. Thus, if "no dole" was an express condition of immigration, immigrants who would come to the U.S. would be the types we want—people who like to take risks, work hard, and be self-reliant and independent—energizing qualities that every society should cherish.

"They'll enter our public schools." Then, prohibit them from doing so. The result would be that they will form their own private, independent schools—and, consequently, provide the nucleus of a new type of person in America: an independent thinker who loves knowledge for its own sake, unlike the public-school student, who simply learns how to memorize and obey.

"They'll take jobs away from Americans." Every American who works today does so under the assumption that he can be replaced with a worker who has moved from another state. All that open immigration would do is open the market even more. But with one big benefit—the new spending by immigrants would open up a wealth of new employment opportunities in the businesses that would have to open or expand to meet the new economic demands.

"They'll dump their products on Americans." Then, retaliate by dumping your products on Americans or on foreigners—consumers will love it! More important, when a person opens a business, he does so under certain risks. One of these risks is that someone else might satisfy the consumers better than other sellers—and that this might happen through low prices or even free goods being given to consumers. If a businessman does not want to take that risk, then he should not go into business.

"They'll get their governments to subsidize their reduced goods." Again, this is a risk that exists in the business world, even domestically. Unfortunately, we live in a world in which people permit their governments to plunder them in order to give a dole to others, including businessmen. No one forces someone to open a business. If a person does not want to take the risk of a government giving a competitor a dole, then there is a simple solution: do not open the business.

"Millions of people will immediately move to the United States." Perhaps. But we must first keep in mind that U.S. government import restrictions create miserable economic conditions in many countries that encourage people to want to emigrate. Once those restrictions are lifted, there is a probability that with the increased economic prosperity in foreign countries, many would-be emigrants would choose to stay at home among friends and family. But if millions did come, great! History has shown that cheap labor, like cheap goods, is a tremendous economic boon to the people of a society. Give us your tired, huddled masses yearning to breathe free—and watch economic prosperity here soar!

Trade restrictions and immigration restrictions are one of the most abominable features of American society today. They have brought impoverishment to millions of poor people—both domestic and foreign. And they violate one of the most fundamental precepts of a free society—the right to do what you want with your money and your life. The times call for leadership—and the American people should lead the world by forcing their government officials to unilaterally lift all trade and immigration controls—and, ultimately, by constitutionally prohibiting American government officials from ever imposing them again.

Jacob G. Hornberger is founder and president of The Future of Freedom Foundation. This essay appeared in the November 1994 issue of Freedom Daily, *published by The Future of Freedom Foundation.*

2

Free Trade, Managed Trade, and the State

by Richard M. Ebeling

"T he principle of free trade is non-interference," wrote the English classical economist Nassau Senior in 1828. "It is to suffer every man to employ his industry in the manner which he thinks most advantageous, without a pretense on the part of the legislator to control or direct his operations."

The advocates of free trade in the 19th century argued that the direction of production and the allocation of resources was best left to the private decisions of the individual members of society rather than to be entrusted to the commands of the state. They explained that each man knows his own circumstances better and can more fully appreciate profitable opportunities than any government bureaucrat assigned the task of performing these duties.

"What is the species of domestic industry which his capital can employ, and of which the produce is likely to be of the greatest value, every individual, it is evident, can, in his local situation, judge much better than any statesman or lawgiver can do for him," said Adam Smith in *The Wealth of Nations*. "The statesman, who should attempt to direct private people in which manner they ought to employ their capitals, would not only load himself with a most unnecessary attention, but assume an authority which could safely be trusted, not only to no single person, but to no council or senate, and which would nowhere be so dangerous as in the hands of a man who had folly and presumption enough to fancy himself fit to exercise it."

And the free traders were insistent on emphasizing that whenever the state interfered with freedom of trade, the benefits that might accrue to the recipient of the protection from competition were always made at the expense of other members of society.

"If one individual, or one class, can call in the aid of the [political] authority to ward off the effects of competition, it acquires a privilege to the prejudice and at the cost of the whole community," insisted the French classical-liberal economist Jean-Baptiste Say in 1821. "It can then make sure of profits not altogether due to the productive services rendered, but composed in part of an actual tax upon consumers for its private profit. . . . Moreover, arbitrary regulations are extremely flattering to the vanity of men in power, as giving them an air of wisdom and foresight, and confirming their authority, which seems to derive additional importance from the frequency of its exercise."

Over several decades in the early 19th century, the arguments of the free-trade advocates gained more and more adherents, first in England and then slowly throughout the rest of Europe and the civilized world.

And what did the free-trade era of the 19th century produce? A wondrous epoch of liberty and prosperity. It was the era of what the German economist Gustav Stolper referred to in his book *This Age of Fable* (1942) as the three freedoms:

> They were: freedom of movement of men, for goods, and for money. Everyone could leave his country when he wanted and travel or migrate wherever he pleased without a passport. The only European country that demanded passports (not even visas!) was Russia. . . . Who wanted to travel to Russia anyway? . . . There were still customs barriers on the European continent, it is true. But the vast British Empire was free-trade territory open to all in free competition, and several other European countries, such as the Netherlands, Belgium, Scandinavia, came close to free trade. . . . Whether a bit higher or a bit lower, tariffs never checked the free flow of goods. All they effected was some minor price changes, presumably mirroring some vested interests. . . . And the most natural of all was the freedom of movement of money. Year in, year out, billions were invested by the great European Powers in foreign countries, European and non-Europeans. . . . These billions were regarded as safe investments with attractive yields, desirable for creditors as

well as debtors, with no doubts about the eventual return of both interest and principle. . . . The interest paid on these foreign investments became an integral part of the national income of the great industrial Powers, protected not only by their political and military might but—more strongly—by the general, unquestioned acceptance of the fundamental capitalist principles: sanctity of treaties, abidance by internal law, and restraint of governments from interference in business.

In the euphoria of this epoch of advancing human freedom and commercial liberty, the proponents of free trade saw only an endless road of growing prosperity and peace. Said the French liberal economist Frederic Passy in the 1860s:

> Some day all barriers will fall; some day mankind, constantly united by continuous transactions, will form just one work-shop, one market, and one family. . . . And this is . . . the grandeur, the truth, the nobility, I might say the holiness of the free-trade doctrine; by the prosaic but effective pressure of [economic] interest it tends to make justice and harmony prevail in the world.

The depoliticizing of economic intercourse among the citizens of the various nations of the world—the privatizing of trade and commerce globally—it needs recalling, was seen by the free traders not only as the path to productive efficiency and rising standards of living through an expanding internationalization of the division of labor and increasing world-wide competition. No. It was also seen as an effective avenue for minimizing the causes of conflict and war among the nations of the world. In 1850, Richard Cobden, the great leader of the English free-trade movement, explained this in a speech:

> When I advocated free trade, do you suppose I did not see its relation to the present question [of war and peace], or that I advocated free trade merely because it would give us a little more occupation in this or that pursuit? No; I believed free trade would have a tendency to unite mankind in the bonds of peace, and it was that, more than any pecuniary consideration, which sustained and actuated me, as my friends know, in that struggle.

International freedom of trade would increasingly make na-tions interdependent. The nations of the world would become the mutual buyers of each other's consumer goods and purchasers of each other's resources and raw materials. The interest income earned by the creditor nations would be the result of the capital supplied to the poorer (in savings) nations; and the productive and profitable investment of that imported capital would accelerate the debtor country's economic development and rise out of poverty. Expanding global competition would not be a rivalry for political power and plunder, but, instead, the peaceful competition of the marketplace in which "victory" and "conquest" became a benign striving among private individuals for economic profits through a better satisfaction of the wants of consumers in comparison to the offers of one's rivals. Success or failure in winning a greater share of the world's business would no longer be "affairs of state," but, instead, the private affairs of individuals pursuing their own personal and peaceful interests, receiving neither subsidy nor protection at the expense of their fellow citizens.

How different is our world of the 20th century in comparison to that of the generations of the 19th century? In the 19th century, the guiding idea was, in the words of Wilhelm Röpke, "the [classical] liberal principle that economic affairs should be free from political direction, the principle of a thorough separation between the spheres of the government and the economy." In our century, the exact opposite has become the dominant idea. Nothing in the 20th century has been considered outside the interests and the concerns of the state. Governments have assigned themselves the role and obligation to interfere everywhere and with everything.

In his 1921 volume, *The Fruits of Victory*, Norman Angell explained:

> The wearing down of the distinction between the citizen and the state, and the inroads upon the sacro-sanctity of private property and individual enterprise, make every citizen much more dependent upon his state, much more a part of it. Control of foreign trade so largely by the state has made international trade less a matter of processes maintained by individuals who disregard their nationality, and more a matter of arrangements between states, in which the non-political individual activity tends to disappear.

Neither men, money nor goods pass across the borders of the world's nations without the inspection, approval, and control of the state. Our lives and our property have become the possessions of the state in which the accident of birth has placed us. The purchase and sale of every commodity and raw material among the citizens of different countries are, once again, affairs of state, matters of government-measured and government-manipulated national income, employment, and output. The exportation or importation of the most minute and insignificant items of consumer desire or productive application has been elevated to concerns of the highest levels of political decision-making and deliberation.

The arrival of the smallest child or the most ordinary adult into one nation from another raises issues of national survival and economic well-being in the eyes of the state. The most innocent choice to invest one's wealth and savings in one part of the world instead of some other generates pensive debate and political consternation for those in the higher reaches of the state's bureaucracy who claim the right to determine how people may invest and dispose of that which is the result of their own effort and energy.

We have been again reduced to a state of increasing servitude from which the classical-liberal revolution of ideas in the 18th and 19th century was meant to liberate us. And with the latest international-trade policy proposals of the Clinton administration, we are headed towards more bondage at the hands of the state.

Part II

In 1836, the English classical liberal Henry Fairbairn looked into the future and this is what he saw:

> Seeing then, that in the natural order of things the triumph of Free Trade principles is now inevitable, magnificent indeed are the prospects that are opening for mankind. Nations will become united in the golden bands of peace; science, liberty and abundance will reign among the inhabitants of the earth; nations will no longer be seen to descend and decline, human life will become prolonged and refined; years will become centuries in the development of the blessings of existence; and even now the eye can reach to the age when one language, one religion, and one nation alone will be existing in the world.

One can only wonder if Mr. Fairbairn's liberal spirit, but no doubt English prejudice, made him presume that the one language would be English, the one religion Anglican, and the one nation the British Empire. But while some of the 19th-century's liberals may have allowed themselves to be excessively carried away with flights of fancy, it remained very much a fact that the success of free-trade ideas transformed the world of the last century.

11

In 1899, the liberal economist C.F. Bastable could write in his book *The Commerce of Nations*:

> One of the most striking features of modern times is the growth of international relations of ever-increasing complexity and influence. . . . This more intimate connexion is reflected in all the different sides of social activity. International law, that two hundred years ago was almost wholly confined to the discussion of war and its effects, now contains a goodly series of chapters treating of the conduct of nations during peace. . . . Literature, Science and Art have all been similarly affected; their followers are engaged in keenly watching the progress of their favorite pursuits in other countries. . . .
>
> But, as might be expected, it is in the sphere of material relations that the increase in international solidarity has been most decisively marked.
>
> The barriers that in former ages impeded the free passage of men and goods from country to country have been—it cannot unfortunately be said removed, but very much diminished; and more particularly during the last fifty years the extraordinary development and improvement of transport agencies both by land and sea have gone far towards obliterating the retarding effects of legislative restraints and national prejudices. . . . In spite of temporary checks and drawbacks, the broad fact stands beyond dispute, that the transfer of human beings from country to country which is known as "migration," as also the similar movement of goods described as "commerce," is not merely expanding, but, if periods sufficiently lengthy for fair comparison are taken, expanding at an accelerated rate.

Free trade among nations and fairly unregulated free enterprise in domestic policy had made the world of the 19th century a time of individual liberty, economic prosperity, and almost a century of relative peace in Europe from the defeat of Napoleon in 1815 to the outbreak of the First World War in 1914. At the dawn of the 20th century, Professor Bastable was concerned that "were we to confine attention to the last twenty years, it would be hardly possible to escape the impression that protection was likely to be the system of the immediate future" because of growing protectionist policies in Imperial Germany, the United States and some of the self-ruling dominions of the British Empire during the last two decades of the 19th century. But he was still confident that while "improvement may be slow, and there have been and will be periods of reaction . . . we can hardly doubt that . . . there will be a fresh effort to gain commercial liberty. . . . [T]here is no likelihood that nations will permanently endure the loss that restriction inflicts on them."

But all such hopes of a return to the path of free trade were killed on the battlefields of World War I. Because in the pursuit of total victory, each of the belligerent governments resorted to total war; and with total war came the total state. German economist Gustav Stolper explained the consequences:

> Just as the war for the first time in history established the principle of universal military service, so for the first time in history it brought national economic life in all its branches and activities to the support and service of state policies—made it effectively subordinate to the state. . . . Not supply and demand, but the dictatorial fiat of the state determined economic relationships—production, consumption, wages, costs of living. . . . [A]t the same time, and for the first time, the state made itself responsible for the physical welfare of its citizens; it guaranteed food and clothing not only for the army in the field but the civilian population. . . .

And what began in the war was continued in the years that followed. Because despite the end of the war, state control and interference into economic affairs were not reduced to their pre-war levels. To the contrary, the period between the two world wars saw state power massively increase. Indeed, by the 1930s, there was not one major country devoted to and practicing the principles of classical liberalism—the principles of individual liberty, free-market capitalism and free trade. As the Swedish economist Gustav Cassel lamented in 1927, "The whole world today is engaged in finding out all sorts of devices to restrict the free division of labor and render its application less profitable" through the imposition of various trading prohibitions, regulations, and controls.

But these restrictions on international trade were the logical consequence of the new ideology regarding the domestic affairs of each of the world's major nations. This ideology was the belief that the state had to become the predominate arbiter and planner of economic affairs. And once the state took on the responsibility for managing and guiding the internal economic affairs of its subjects, barriers to international trade were soon required to follow. In 1944, the Austrian economist Ludwig von Mises explained why:

13

A nation's policy forms an integral whole. Foreign policy and domestic policy are closely linked together, they condition each other. Economic nationalism is the corollary of present-day domestic policies of government interference with business and of national planning, as free trade was the complement of domestic economic freedom. When the domestic market is not to some extent insulated from the foreign market, there can be no question of government control. . . . The trend toward [protectionism] is essentially a trend of domestic policies; it is the outcome of the endeavors to make the state paramount in economic matters.

If governments choose a course of domestic interventionism and control, interference with international trade inevitably follows. Privileges and regulations to benefit producers within a country are constantly threatened by foreign competition under free trade; hence, to guarantee those privileges for domestic producers, the government has to impose trade barriers against foreign imports. When trade unions are allowed to use the strike threat to push wages above world-market levels, and when welfare benefits make unemployment a reasonably comfortable way of life, immigration restrictions have to be imposed to prevent those in other countries from entering the nation and offering their labor services at a lower wage and filling the jobs shunned by the domestic labor force. When governments resort to inflation to finance their domestic expenditures, the result is monetary nationalism manifested in government paper currencies and foreign-exchange controls and regulations.

In the 20th century, the politicization of domestic economic activities, therefore, has led to the politicization of the international economic order. To secure markets and prices for domestic producers, governments are tempted to threaten or wage trade wars with other countries, with import tariffs and export subsidies being among the chief economic weapons, as well as a host of non-tariff restrictions such as quotas, prohibitions, licensing, and technical and domestic-content requirements. Manipulation of the value of their respective currencies on the foreign-exchange markets also serves as an economic weapon by which governments try to influence the amounts of imports and exports and, hence, the market shares and profits to be earned by privileged sectors of the domestic economy.

There is only one way out of this "economic armaments race," as the Swiss economist William Rappard once referred to it in the 1930s: a path of non-intervention in domestic affairs—the unregulated, uncontrolled free market. Otherwise, economic conflicts among nations will always threaten to degenerate into global economic warfare. "Government control of business engenders conflicts for which no peaceful solution can be found," Ludwig von Mises emphasized long ago. "All the oratory of the advocates of government omnipotence cannot annul the fact that there is but one system that makes for durable peace: a free market economy. Government control leads to economic nationalism and this results in conflict."

Unfortunately, this path to economic peace and prosperity is not the one that the Clinton administration is bent upon following. Rather, its stated intentions in both domestic and international trade point in the direction of an increasing economic armaments race, with economic warfare on the horizon.

Part III

American economist Francis Walker observed in 1887:

> Protectionism is purely and highly socialistic. Its purpose is so to operate upon individual choices and aims, so to influence private enterprise and the investments of capital, as to secure the building up, within the country concerned, of certain branches of production which could not be carried on, or would grow but slowly, under the rule of competition and individual initiative. With this object in view, government begins by preventing the citizen from buying where he can buy cheapest; it compels him to pay ten, thirty or fifty percent advance, it may be upon the prices at which he could otherwise purchase; it even assumes to make existing industries support the industries which are thus called into being. Not incidentally, but primarily and of purpose, it affects vitally every man's industrial conditions and relations.

The proponents of managed trade in the Clinton administration would surely balk at Professor Walker's accusation that what they advocate is a form of socialism. After all, they might respond, when speaking of the changes in post-Soviet Russia and in the former Soviet-bloc countries in Eastern Europe, they constantly say they advocate the establishment of a free market. And in the controversy over the North American Free Trade Agreement, spokesmen for the administration are equally adamant that they desire to see a greater openness for trading opportunities among these three economies on our continent.

15

Yet, in spite of their rhetoric and lip service of advocacy for open doors for world trade, their goal is not free trade. Their view of trade among nations is guided by the following ideas:

1) International trade is not between private individuals searching out advantageous gains from exchange, but rather an economic war among nation-states in which the victories for one country require the defeat of another;

2) It is in the power of governments to forecast the world economic trends of the future and devise systems of import restrictions and technological and production subsidies for the artificial creation of patterns of comparative advantage that will assure that America gains a permanent edge in the manufacturing and sale of certain desirable lines of production;

3) If other governments restrict the importation of American goods into their countries, it is the duty of the United States government to use various weapons of economic warfare to force those foreign markets to open to American competition.

Let us look at each of these ideas and evaluate their validity and consequences.

The view that international trade is economic warfare among nations:

Contrary to the Clinton view, international trade is merely an extension of the idea of the division of labor within a country to the residents of different geographical locations separated from each other by the drawing of political boundaries on the face of a map. By expanding the arena of trade to encompass more people around the world, all participants are made better off. The enlarged market enables an intensification of specialization to take advantage of the various and sundry skills and capabilities of a greater number of potential producers and traders in more parts of the globe. The increased specialization in the expanded market widens the field of competitors to assure that the prices at which goods are available in the global market are the lowest at which producers are capable of offering them to the consuming public.

In the arena of free exchange, all traders are gainers and none are losers. The decision to exchange one commodity or service for another demonstrates that both participants to the exchange view themselves as being better off because what induces them to give one thing for another is the following mutual belief: what they are giving up is of a lower value in comparison to what they obtain; otherwise, they would not voluntarily trade away what is originally in their possession.

But in an open market, individual competitors sometimes discover that they are unable to match the better prices or product

16

qualities of their foreign competitors. And rather than accept the loss of market share or desired profit margins to those who can provide consumers at better terms than themselves, they turn to the state for assistance. They call upon the political authority to limit the liberty of the foreign seller from offering his wares in the home country and deny the consumers in the home country the greater freedom to purchase from him who offers the preferred goods at the more attractive terms.

The advocate of protection from the foreign competitors cloaks his special pleading in the rhetoric of the patriot who insists that his industry is essential to the national welfare or for the preservation of employment. But, in fact, the only welfare that is at stake is his own. And he wishes to sacrifice the welfare of others for his own benefit, because for his market share to be preserved or his profitableness to be maintained through various protectionist restrictions, the welfare of the individual consumers in his country must be reduced by their inability to buy the cheaper or better product from the foreign seller. And the welfare of the producers in the foreign country is diminished since they are denied the opportunity to consummate trades that would have offered the more attractive return if not for the trade restrictions.

It is the intervention of the state into the nexus of exchange that now makes international trade a battlefield upon which economic wars are fought. Victory in the arena of global trade is now partly determined by the use of weapons of taxation, coercion, and prohibition: thou shalt not sell your goods in the U.S. without first paying a toll meant to secure a minimum-guaranteed price for the domestic producers; thou shalt not sell your goods in the U.S. unless they contain a certain "domestic content" of American raw materials or have been manufactured with the assistance of a certain number of American workers; thou shalt not sell your goods at all in the U.S., because the market is to be the privileged preserve of those domestic producers with the political clout to close the market completely to foreign competition.

War is the use of force to obtain desired ends without having to obtain the voluntary consent of those who possess that which is wanted. And in international trade, it is only the state that can transform peaceful intercourse among the occupants of the world into a violent combat of political weaponry for the "capture" of customers and the "defeat" of rivals.

The Clinton administration is imbued with the spirit of the managed economy—socialism. The notion of leaving the market to its own development and outcomes is intolerable to its conception of social justice and belief in socially engineering economic results. The administration, therefore, must battle against the patterns the market would naturally take on if the government were not to intervene, and this necessarily results in foreign suppliers being aggressed upon in the combat, as well.

If the state is to determine the desired direction of domestic economic development, then it is also the case that as part of the achievement of that end, the pattern of imports and exports must be managed too. Investments in certain types of technologies, methods of production, and lines of production that the government decides are necessary for national economic well-being require not only tax breaks, subsidies, and "partnerships" between the government and private firms, they also require that foreign producers and suppliers not be allowed to undermine the domestic policy goals by offering products and technologies that American consumers would rather buy instead.

Barriers and limits to entry into the U.S. market must follow. At the same time, the sustaining of these domestic economic patterns also requires that the government support the exporting of those goods and services that are both consistent with and a part of the domestic policy plan for managed economic development.

The government then is in an economic war with both its own citizens and those of other countries. It battles against its own citizens, because some must be taxed, regulated, or denied production and consumption opportunities so the state's goals for a managed economy can be obtained. And foreign suppliers are aggressed against because the government denies them the right to enter peacefully the American market without molestation; coming through the door, they are mugged in the form of tariffs, quotas, and domestic-content requirements.

International trade only becomes economic warfare when the state intervenes into the economic affairs of its own citizens and those of other countries. The economic warfare, however, is not between nation-states, but instead that of nation-states against private citizens. The confusion in clearly seeing this is due to the common use of linguistic shorthand in referring to the economic relationships between "America" and "Europe" or "Japan."

But it is ultimately individuals who supply and demand, who produce and consume. It is impossible for the government to institute any policy other than the one of providing equal protection of each individual's rights to life and property without infringing on some people's rights to bestow privileges and favors on others. And to the extent that the state goes beyond this limited role of providing equal protection of rights before the law, it declares and initiates war against its own citizens.

Part IV

"The Protectionist creed rises like a weed in every soil," lamented the English classical economist Walter Bagehot in the 1880s. "Every nation wishes prosperity for some conspicuous industry. At what cost to the consumer, by what hardship to less conspicuous industries, that prosperity is obtained, it does not care. Indeed, it hardly knows, it will not read, it will never apprehend the refined reasons which prove those evils and show how great they are; the visible picture of the smoking chimneys absorbs the whole mind."

While the imagery of the smoking chimney may be inconsistent with the environmental consciousness of the Clinton administration, Bagehot's lament can be echoed in our own times in terms of the mind-set that dominates the thinking of the president and those who design policy options in the departments in Washington. Their conception of managed trade focuses upon the desired success of targeted industries viewed as essential to the nation's prosperity in their conception of the global combat amongst the countries of the world. The cost to the consuming public in terms of higher taxes to subsidize preferred industries or in diminished trading opportunities because of limits on international freedom of exchange matters little to those in the Washington halls of power. What matters is that they see rise in front of them those industries and employments that they view as the most advantageous and attractive.

If the first error behind the thinking of the Clinton administration on the issue of international trade is their view of international trade as a war between nation-states, their second error is the one that serves as the philosophical underpinning for rationalizing the ability for and desirability of managed trade. Let us look at it more closely:

Governments can forecast world economic trends and should construct policies to create desired comparative advantages for American industry:

In spite of the failure of socialist central planning in Eastern Europe and the former Soviet Union, the planning mentality is alive and well in Clinton's Washington. There exists the belief that it is possible for the government to estimate reasonably the direction and form of future technological and industrial developments in the world and construct a plan of action to assure that America comes out the winner in the international game of trade.

Actually, it is impossible to anticipate successfully the future of technological discovery or innovations for improvements in the methods of producing goods for the market. Every such judgment

19

about the future shape of things to come is made from the standpoint of the knowledge and information in existence today.

But as philosopher of science Karl Popper pointed out long ago, it is a contradiction to speak about tomorrow's knowledge today. We can never speak about what we will know tomorrow but only about what we think tomorrow may be like from the perspective of what we already know today. Tomorrow's knowledge cannot be known until tomorrow comes, because part of what we know tomorrow will be the result of the experiences we have as time passes and the creative new ideas that people come up with on the basis of those experiences.

Thus, unless we assume that we possess perfect knowledge of the future, all judgments about the future—including new technologies, innovations, patterns of consumer demands and the strategies of competitors—are incomplete and personal estimates about what the future might hold in store from the perspective of the present.

I remember as a teenager coming across an old copy of *Popular Science* published shortly after the Second World War. The issue was devoted to what life would be like in America in the 1970s. The cover showed a suburban home with a white picket fence, with mom and the children waving good-bye to dad as he went off to work—in his one-man helicopter. The articles talked about the various home conveniences and appliances that the future held in store for the average American family.

But the one thing that was not talked about or even hinted at was the potentials of the personal computer and its revolutionizing effect on home and business life. Why? Because the microchip had not yet been invented and, therefore, all the projections about life in the late 20th century were incomplete.

The writers of the articles wrote their stories about the future under the constraint of the knowledge they possessed at the time in the late 1940s. It was impossible for them to construct the uses of a technology that had not yet been invented in the minds of some men, and, therefore, they were not able to conceive of its applications, because they could not image possibilities that would have to wait for the creation of the microchip.

To manage the economy requires The Planner to make the plans of a multitude of others subordinate to his own. And as Austrian economist Friedrich A. Hayek explained, this means that economic development is constrained and limited to what The Planner knows and can understand, since everyone else's plans must conform to and be confined within the bounds of The Planner's overarching plan. If the state taxes some in the society to subsidize the activities of others, those who are taxed are constricted in their own actions to the extent that their income has been reduced by the tax. The resources that might otherwise have been used and possibly applied in creative and unknowable ways are taken from their hands. Creativity, technological innovation, and economic progress are limited to what The Planner sees as possible and worthwhile to support and fund.

The government-business partnerships and high-tech subsidy programs for America advocated by the Clinton administration are really proposals for a political centralization of the discovery and application of knowledge, and they channel their development according to the judgments of those who man the bureaucracies in Washington. They propose to figure out where the industrial innovations of the future are likely to be. Then, based upon their judgment about the shape of things to come, they aim to give shelter to American firms they want to be on the world market first with these new technologies and, thus, to preempt that new corner of the global market before anyone else can fill it.

What is not discussed in these grandiose schemes for America's industrial future are the costs of undertaking them. The costs involve more than the corruption that is likely to occur as special interests lobby for a fraction of the tax- and subsidy-plunder. The costs also involve more than the loss of economic liberty, as those individuals not on the receiving end of the government largess are restricted in their choices by both regulations and tax burdens to bolster and support the privileged sectors of the economy.

The costs also include the loss of all the innovations and creative possibilities that will not materialize or which will be delayed from coming to fruition, because those who might have come up with them will not have the income and financial wherewithal to realize them.

What idea equal to the microchip will we not benefit from because those in whose minds such an idea might have germinated will be denied the market opportunities that would have acted as the incentive for them to think such creative thoughts? Because the income, profits, and wealth that could have been theirs from such creative thinking will be denied them by the state's manipulation of the market, they may turn their efforts to less original ideas. And the world will have lost a profoundly important "might have been" as a consequence.

But precisely because it is a "might have been," its importance will remain stillborn. It is an example of Frederic Bastiat's famous example of "what is seen and what is unseen." What will be seen are

the industrial and technological projects subsidized into existence
due to the actions of the state. What "might have been," instead, will
never be known precisely because the state assumed to know better,
to see the future more clearly, rather than to allow each man to follow
his own vision of a better future for himself and others through
peaceful and voluntary transactions in the marketplace.

The market niches that the government creates for American
industries through managed trade will be the industrial equivalents
of the hothouse in which, under artificial conditions, plants are
grown in an environment naturally hostile to their development.
Their maintenance and further development will depend upon the
continuance of the governmental policies that have brought them
into existence. They will be the 20th- and 21st-centuries' versions of
the 19th-century argument for protecting the "infant industry."

Protectionists in the last century would often argue that an
undeveloped country could not afford free trade until it was as
industrially developed as its more technologically advanced trading
partners. Only then, when the underdeveloped country was sufficiently developed behind high tariff barriers to protect it from cheaper
suppliers from abroad, could it afford to lower its trade walls and deal
on an equal basis with its commercial neighbors. The only problem
was that the infant industries never sufficiently grew up; they always
clamored for continuing protection from their foreign competitors.

Having fostered the artificial emergence and development of
certain high-tech industries and employment opportunities requir-
ing particular government-subsidized labor skills, the proponents of
managed trade will always find arguments for perpetuating the
"temporary" taxing and tariff privileges needed for initially establishing these strategic positions in the global market. The American
taxpayer and consumer will be permanently burdened with the costs
imposed by those who believe that they possess the knowledge and
wisdom to know the industrial and economic structure most desirable for America's future.

Part V

In the 1870s, English classical economist Henry Faucett warned:

> I think it cannot be doubted that protection must exert an
> inevitable tendency to foster . . . socialistic demands for State
> assistance. If a people are accustomed as they must be under a
> system of protection, to believe that the prosperity of each
> separate branch of industry depends not so much upon indi-
> vidual energy as upon the amount of protection it can obtain

from the government, there can be no surer way of encouraging the growth of a belief not only that industrial prosperity but that the general social well-being of the country is chiefly to be secured not by individual effort but by State help.

And a few years earlier, the American economist and sociologist William Graham Sumner had pointed out other political consequences that followed from a policy of protectionism:

This continual law making about industry has been prolific of industrial and political mischief. It has tainted our political life with log-rolling, presidential wire-pulling, lobbying, and custom-house politics. It has been intertwined with currency errors all the way along. It has created privileged classes in the free American community, who were saved from the risks and dangers of business to which the rest of us are liable. It has controlled the election of congressmen, and put inferior men in office, whose inferiority has reacted upon the nation in worse and worse legislation.

The Clinton administration's declared policy of managed trade between the United States and the rest of the world will only succeed in intensifying the tendencies which Faucett and Sumner warned about more than a hundred years ago: an increased dependency upon the state by a growing number of sectors of the economy, along with a belief that such dependency is the only path to economic prosperity; and a growing corruption of the political process as more and more groups in the society turn to Washington for favors and privileges, both to gain advantages at the expense of rivals in the marketplace and as a defensive mechanism against the political lobbying efforts of others.

Three errors dominate the Clinton administration's case for managed trade. The first is the belief that international trade is an economic war between nation-states; the belief is that if one nation gains, some other nation must lose.

The second error is the belief that the state has the capacity to anticipate the future direction of technological development and to design policies to assure that American industry will have a permanent edge in the battle for winning world markets against our trading partners.

The third error serves as the pragmatic rationale for a policy of managed trade: *If other governments restrict the importation of American goods into their countries, it is the duty of the U.S. government to use various weapons of economic warfare to force open those foreign markets for American competition.*

It is argued that if, in a world of free trade, another nation closes its market to some or all of American goods, while desiring to sell its own goods in the United States, the U.S. government should put retaliatory pressure on that country to open its market through the imposition of reciprocal tariffs and other trade restrictions.

Writing in the early 19th century, the French classical-liberal economist Jean Baptiste-Say, admitted:

> Undoubtedly, a nation that excludes you from all commercial intercourse with her, does you an injury;—robs you, as far as in her lies, of the benefits of external commerce. . . . But it must not be forgotten that retaliation hurts yourself as well as your rival; that it operates, not defensively against her selfish measures, but offensively against yourself, in the first instance, for the purpose of indirectly attacking her. The only point in question is this, what degree of vengeance you are animated by, and how much will you consent to throw away upon its gratification.

The fact is that the use of reciprocal trade restrictions as a weapon of economic warfare to punish another country for closing its own markets to American exports results in harm to the general American consuming public; raises the cost of various commodities previously purchased from the foreign nation now experiencing American revenge and retaliation; and imposes financial burdens on the import industries in the U.S. no longer able to obtain certain foreign goods on as favorable terms as before the retaliatory trade restrictions were put into place.

Closing a portion or all of the American market to the exports of the foreign country subjected to the wrath of the U.S. government narrows the competitive alternatives available to American consumers. Their set of choices is now limited to those offered by American sellers of various products and those foreign sellers of other countries not affected by the retaliatory trade barriers. The variety of goods, therefore, from which the U.S. consuming public may select is smaller than before. Because some American exporters have been put in a less favorable position due to the foreign country's trade limitations, all other Americans are denied buying opportunities by their own government.

At the same time, prices will now be higher for the particular products upon which there have now been imposed the retaliatory trade restrictions. The segment of the American consuming public that was previously buying the foreign goods in question will now find themselves having to pay higher prices for those commodities. Whether the retaliation takes the form of a tariff or a limit on the quantity of the foreign good now permitted to enter the United States, the good's price will tend to rise. If a tariff has been imposed, the foreign seller will have to sell his good at a higher price to cover his costs (now including a higher import tax) or to retain the rate of return that makes it advantageous to sell the good in the U.S., as opposed to somewhere else. If restrictions are imposed on the quantity that may be sold in the U.S., the total quantity available in the American market will now be smaller, which will tend to result in a higher price. Because U.S. export "X" is not permitted to be sold in the foreign country in question, American consumers will now be faced with higher prices and smaller quantities of imports "Y" and "Z" purchased from that other country.

Also, the segments of the American import industry that sell the goods now under retaliatory restriction will find themselves with the burden of having to pay more for the goods they purchase from the foreign seller and then having to try to sell those goods to American consumers under less competitive terms than before. Because an American exporter claims harm, income earners in an unrelated importing sector of the U.S. economy will have to pay for the exporter's misfortune.

Many of these effects remain hidden from view by governments' arguing in terms of "our" nation being harmed by "theirs." But once we stop thinking in this aggregative and collectivist manner and ask who is harmed or helped in terms of particular individuals or groups of individuals, the consequences are seen to be more complicated than the simplistic categories of "them" versus "us."

The real effect of trade retaliation is something more like the following: The government of Boobistan prohibits the sale of American bicycles in Boobistan, resulting in fewer foreign sales for American bicycle manufacturers and higher prices for bicycles in Boobistan to benefit Boobistani bicycle manufacturers at the expense of Boobistani consumers. Therefore, in retaliation, the U.S. government imposes a tariff or prohibits the sale of Boobistani dingbats in America. American consumers of Boobistani dingbats now find themselves paying more and buying a smaller quantity of this valued commodity, and the American import companies that make their living selling Boobistani dingbats find it more difficult to make a living in this line of business.

25

Who gains from this retaliation against Boobistan? Not American bicycle manufacturers—they are still locked out of the Boobistani market. Not American consumers or importers of Boobistani dingbats—they bear the negative effects we have just explained. If the retaliation has taken the form of a higher import tariff on dingbats, the U.S. government may or may not gain greater tax revenues, depending on how many Boobistani dingbats are now brought into the United States at the higher tariff. The only gainers are the manufacturers of the American version of dingbats, who now face less price and quantity competition from their Boobistani rivals, and the sellers of goods that are bought by American consumers as substitutes for the now more expensive dingbats.

But what do dingbats—and helping American dingbat manufacturers to earn higher profits—have to do with the lost sales and lower profits experienced by American bicycle manufacturers caused by Boobistani trade barriers? Nothing. They simply provide the rationale for American dingbat producers to lobby for restrictions of Boobistani imports. And they enable American politicians to "act tough" with Boobistan, thereby looking good in the eyes of American voters who have been led to believe that Boobistan is destroying American jobs because "they" won't buy "our" bicycles.

Might not Boobistan back down and eliminate its trade barriers against American bicycles under the threat of retaliation against their export trade in dingbats? Yes, they might. And the proponents of trade-war brinkmanship often use this as an argument to defend the use of the retaliatory threat.

But the danger of accepting this rationale for one of the tools of economic warfare among governments is that it legitimizes the idea that the state is responsible for and has the right to intervene in the exchange relationships between their own citizens and the citizens and governments of other nations. It accepts the nationalization of international trade, because it accepts the premise that among the state's duties is supervision of the patterns of terms of trade among the producers and consumers of the world.

Furthermore, if the Boobistani government doesn't blink first, the retaliatory restrictions must then be put in place—if the threatening government is not to lose credibility both at home and abroad. And this creates the risk that Boobistan might counter-retaliate, setting in motion a spiral of expanding trade barriers and the disintegration of an increasing portion of the international division of labor.

Unfortunately, this is the path that the Clinton administration is threatening to lead us down even further than we have already come. And the further we travel down this path, the more difficult it will become to retrace our steps and return to the high road of individual liberty and free trade.

Richard M. Ebeling is the Ludwig von Mises Professor of Economics at Hillsdale College in Hillsdale, Michigan, and serves as vice president of academic affairs for The Future of Freedom Foundation. This essay appeared as a five-part series in the August 1993 through December 1993 issues of Freedom Daily, *published by The Future of Freedom Foundation.*

3

A Capitalist Looks at Free Trade

by William L. Law

Protectionists seeking relief from the rigors of foreign competition bring to mind Milton Friedman's dictum, "The great enemies of free enterprise are businessmen and intellectuals—businessmen because they want socialism for themselves and free enterprise for everyone else; intellectuals, because they want free enterprise for themselves and socialism for everyone else."

I speak from personal experience. Baseball-glove leather was the principal product of our firm until 1957 when ball gloves of Japanese manufacture appeared and ultimately gained seventy percent of the United States' market. Today, we tan no baseball-glove leather. Sentiment in the ball-glove industry at that time was very strong for protective action. I investigated the matter in some depth and found that I could not in good faith urge protectionist action on my political representatives; such action would have been wrong economically, politically, and morally.

My sentiments stem from the fact that I look upon myself not as a tanner whose product is leather, but as a capitalist whose product is profit. That climate most beneficial to capitalists—and to workers—is one in which there exists a minimum of governmental interference.

The protectionist argument is almost as widespread today as it was two hundred years ago when Adam Smith in his treatise *An*

Inquiry into the Nature and Causes of The Wealth of Nations so brilliantly demonstrated its fallacies. Fortunately, we have the work of Smith and his many successors, plus the empirical lessons on the benefits of free trade—our fifty states united in one common market are a notable example—to demonstrate the advantages of free exchange.

No improvement can be made on Smith's understanding:

> It is the highest impertinence of kings and ministers, to pretend to watch over the economy of private people, and to restrain their expense, either by sumptuary laws, or by prohibiting the importation of foreign luxuries. They are themselves always, and without any exception, the greatest spendthrifts in society. Let them look well after their own expense, and they may safely trust private people with theirs. If their own extravagance does not ruin the state, that of their subjects never will. . . .
>
> To give the monopoly of the home market to the produce of domestic industry . . . must, in almost all cases be either a useless or a hurtful regulation. If the produce of domestic industry can be bought there as cheap as that of foreign industry, the regulation is evidently useless. If it cannot, it must generally be hurtful.
>
> It is the maxim of every prudent master of a family never to attempt to make at home what it will cost him more to make than to buy. The tailor does not attempt to make his own shoes, but buys them of a shoemaker. The shoemaker does not attempt to make his own clothes, but employs a tailor. The farmer attempts to make neither the one nor the other, but employs those different artificers. All of them find it in their interests to employ their whole industry in a way in which they have some advantage over their neighbors, and to purchase with a part of its produce, or what is the same thing, with the price of a part of it, whatever else they have occasion for. What is prudence in the conduct of every private family, can scarce be folly in that of a great kingdom. . . .
>
> That it was the spirit of monopoly which originally both invented and propagated this [protectionist] doctrine cannot be doubted; and they who first taught it were by no means such fools as they who believed it. In every country it always is and must be the interest of the great body of the people to buy whatever they want of those who sell it cheapest. The proposition is so very manifest, that it seems ridiculous to take any pains to prove it; nor could it ever have been called in question

had not the interested sophistry of merchants and manufacturers confounded the common sense of mankind.

The "sophistry" of which Smith speaks is in essence that being advanced today by protectionists: "The U.S. is a high-wage country; its industry is unable to compete with that in low-wage countries; imports are increasing, and unless remedial measures are adopted, our industries will be destroyed and large-scale unemployment will ensue."

But fortunately, we have the rationale and arguments for free trade.

We trade to obtain goods that are either unobtainable domestically, such as chrome ore, diamonds, and teak wood, or that can be obtained more cheaply abroad, such as baseball gloves or textiles.

And free trade raises wages! Trade between individuals, between states, between nations is beneficial, and far from reducing the living standards of the participants, greatly improves them. And the country with the freest trade policy enjoys the maximum advantage.

I repeat: *free trade raises wages!* Those who think otherwise fail to understand that wages in the U.S. are the world's highest for a reason: American industry has the world's highest average capital investment per worker ($125,000) and, therefore, has the highest average productivity per worker. And while we have high wages, because of the multiplier—tools, we also have low labor costs!

Certainly, labor-intensive industries, i.e., textiles, find it difficult to compete inside a capital-intensive country. After all, a Chinese worker with minimal capital—a needle—and working for $20 a week, will produce handmade lace at a lower cost than an American worker using the same needle and receiving $200 a week. While their productivity will be the same, the Chinese labor cost will be one-tenth of the U.S. cost.

But give the American worker a giant mechanical shovel and, at the world's highest wage, he will produce the world's cheapest coal. With advanced technology, workers will produce the lowest-cost coal, wheat, jet aircraft and countless other goods. And so, we import lace and ball gloves and petroleum, and we export jet planes and wheat and chemicals. To attempt to "retaliate" against lower costs in certain foreign industries is an exercise in folly.

Moreover, contrary to popular belief, imports don't cause unemployment, nor do immigration or automation. *Unemployment exists only when money wages are arbitrarily raised or held above the market price.*

31

The Great Depression is the classic case of "iatrogenic" unemployment, i.e., induced by the economic doctor. For example, when the stock market crashed in 1929, it precipitated a deflation and concomitant lowering of all prices. Presidents Hoover and Roosevelt, believing in the so-called "purchasing power theory," cooperated with major industrialists and union leaders to do everything in their power to prevent wages from falling—even though prices in general had dropped by one-third from 1929 to 1932! The result was that *twenty-five to thirty percent of the work force was unemployed.* The situation was not ameliorated until 1941 when the government printed massive amounts of money to support the war effort; and instead of trying to support wages, the government took the opposite position and introduced controls to hold wages down. Unemployment soon disappeared and industry expanded.

Unfortunately, a false lesson was learned that war is the health of the economy. (James Baker, secretary of state during the Bush administration, reflected this when he explained why the U.S. government was intervening in the Middle East after the Iraqi invasion of Kuwait: "If you want to sum it up in one word, it's jobs.") The truth, of course, is that war is actually the enemy of prosperity (and freedom) and that full employment is actually the normal condition of a truly free economy.

Protectionism is the age-old road to reduced exports, increased unemployment, lower standards of living, war, and so many other problems associated with government intervention in economic activity. Free trade, on the other hand, is the way to increased exports, full employment, higher standards of living, peace, and so many other benefits associated with economic freedom.

William L. Law is chairman of the board of Cudahy Tanning Company in Cudahy, Wisconsin. This essay appeared in the June 1991 issue of Freedom Daily, *published by The Future of Freedom Foundation.*

4

Free Trade Versus Protectionism

by Richard M. Ebeling

A specter is haunting the economies of the world. It is the specter of protectionism. In one country after the other, cries are heard that international trade, rather than bringing mutual prosperity, imposes economic hardship on some nations so that others may gain. Trading practices among nations are declared to be "unfair." Jobs are supposedly lost through "cheap" imports flooding domestic markets. Balance of trade deficits threaten the financial stability of not only third-world countries, but the United States as well.

And the solutions proposed are the same everywhere: demands are made for the imposition or stiffening of trade restrictions—the raising of barriers in the path of trade among nations. It is claimed that limitations on amounts of foreign supplies entering the domestic market, through either tariffs that make foreign goods more costly or quotas that prohibit the quantities which may be imported, will increase the market share of domestic companies as well as enhance employment opportunities at home.

The reasoning seems straightforward and sensible. However, it suffers from one handicap: *It is dead wrong!* When implemented, protectionist policies bring economic harm, as well as lower standards of living, for the people of every nation choosing to follow this path.

If the protectionist argument is correct—that buying Japanese goods, for example, is harmful to American industry and jobs as a whole—then the same logic would have to imply that importing New Mexico goods is harmful to Texas industry and jobs; and that buying Fort Worth goods is harmful to Dallas industry and jobs. Why does the Japanese-U.S. argument seem plausible, while the Fort Worth-Dallas argument appears suspect? Because people still suffer from the tribal notion that suggests that the accident of a political boundary across the face of a map must imply antagonism between the human beings who live on different sides of that boundary.

International trade is nothing more than an extension of the social division of labor across national borders. And the same advantages that arise from a division of labor between members of the same nation apply among members of different nations. It enables a specialization of skills and abilities, with each member of the world economic community tending to specialize in that line of production in which he has a comparative advantage (a relative superiority) in relation to his trading neighbors.

Through such a division of tasks and activities, the wealth and prosperity of every nation is increased, as compared to a situation in which individuals or nations are required to obtain what they desire through their own efforts, in economic isolation from their fellow men.

But what of the particular charges presently leveled against our foreign trading partners? What about the detrimental effects which supposedly result from the trading policies of other nations? Let us examine some of these charges:

1. *Unfair trading practices.* A number of nations have been accused of unfairly subsidizing the export of goods to America, i.e., at prices which are below their "actual" cost of production.

The world is going through a dramatic technological and economic revolution, with many underdeveloped nations finally entering the industrialized era. Their lower prices often merely reflect their lower costs of production, as they shift into positions in the international division of labor which reflect those areas where their relative economic efficiencies are greatest. As these nations sell more in the United States, they earn the purchasing power to buy more from America. American exports, therefore, increase because the only way for foreigners to buy more from Americans is for Americans to sell more to foreigners.

To the extent that foreign governments do subsidize some products sold in the U.S., this means that Americans are able to buy them below what would have otherwise been the market price. In other words, *we are given a bargain,* a bargain that saves us resources that would have been devoted to the making of more products to pay for what otherwise would have been higher-priced imports. And these resources are now available to make other things that we would not have been able to produce without this bargain. It is the citizens of those other nations who should be outraged since they, not us, have to foot the tax bill to pay for the subsidies.

2. *Foreign products cause loss of jobs.* The charge is made that the sale of foreign goods in America "steals" markets away from American companies, with a resulting loss of jobs in America.

This argument ignores the fact that these foreign goods must be paid for. It is true that jobs in those sectors of the economy which directly compete against certain foreign products may be lost. But other jobs are created in those industries which manufacture goods which foreigners are interested in purchasing from Americans. The sale of foreign goods in America may change the locale and types of employments in the U.S., but it need not result, over time, in any net loss of jobs.

Furthermore, with free trade, Americans end up spending less of their income on certain products because they are bought more cheaply from foreign suppliers. This leaves them with extra dollars with which they are able to increase their demand for other goods on the market. The net effect, therefore, is to stimulate even more employment opportunities than previously existed.

3. *The balance of trade deficit and foreign investment.* The leading issue during the last several years has been the charge that America buys more abroad than it sells, resulting in a trade deficit that threatens the economic stability of the United States.

It is true that in terms of tangible or visible goods, the U.S. has been buying more than it has sold. But this overlooks the overall trade "balance sheet." Instead of buying American commodities with the dollars they have earned, foreign earners of dollars have returned some of them to America in the form of savings in the credit markets, or as direct investment in U.S. industry. The overall balance of payments between the United States and the rest of the world *has balanced.*

When this is pointed out, the concern expressed is that foreigners are "buying up America." "They" will control "us." Actually, however, when the foreign investment is "indirect," i.e., loaned to Americans through the banking system, this merely increases the pool of savings in the United States; and this pool of savings is available to domestic businessmen who desire to expand or improve their plant and equipment. If wisely used, the money borrowed will be paid back, with interest. And, in a few years, the productive capital in America will be greater and more efficient. Industry will still be in "our" hands.

But what if the investment is direct? Won't foreigners "control" America by buying out existing companies or starting up new businesses which successfully compete against American-owned firms? Again, this reflects the collectivist notions of past ages, notions which think of those who belong to other nations—"tribes"— as inherently dangerous enemies.

But those of other nations who invest in America are actually "our" captives—if one wishes to use this form of reasoning. They have invested their savings in America because it has offered the most attractive economic and political environment. Their own fortunes and futures are linked to continuing American prosperity; and they must manage their investments in judicious, market-oriented directions if they are to generate the profits for which they hope.

But what if "they" pulled out? Would that not hurt "us" by disrupting "our" economy? In such a case, the physical plant and equipment remain in America. To "pull out," they would have to find willing buyers. And to do that, they would have to offer attractive prices to prospective buyers. And they would only want to sell out if either the political or economic climate in the U.S. became less attractive as compared to other countries. But are these not the same incentives and motives which guide Americans who invest and save in New York rather than California, or in the U.S. rather than some other country?

While there will always be necessary adjustments to new and changing circumstances, free trade between nations ultimately benefits *all* who participate. Protectionism can only lead us down a road of impoverishment and international commercial tensions. To paraphrase the great 18th-century, free-market thinker David Hume when he criticized the protectionists of his time: Not only as a man, but as an American, I pray for the flourishing commerce of Germany, France, England, and even Japan. Why? Because America's prosperity and economic future are dependent upon the economic prosperity of all of those with whom it trades in the international division of labor.

This essay appeared in the January 1991 issue of Freedom Daily, *published by The Future of Freedom Foundation.*

5

The Tariff Idea

by W.M. Curtiss

One of the fallacies popular throughout the world is the belief that exports are good and imports are bad. If we sell more than we buy, we have a "favorable" balance of trade—and that is supposed to be good. Actually, in a free market there is no such thing as a favorable or unfavorable balance of trade. There is simply a balance.

Trade between nations is not different in this respect from trade between individuals. Suppose you sell a bushel of apples for two dollars. You get two dollars, which you would rather have than the apples; the buyer gets the apples, which he would rather have than two dollars. A perfect balance!

True enough, our exporters may sell goods to English buyers and get sterling exchange. They may spend this money in France or Germany rather than in England, so that the flow of goods is not directly between England and America. But the same might be true in the trade of apples for dollars. With your two dollars, you probably will buy something from a third party rather than from the man who bought the apples.

If we are to buy, we must sell. If we are to export, we must import. It is just that simple. Erecting barriers against imports is just another way of cutting down our exports. There will still be a balance, but at a lower level.

Actually, tariffs have nothing to do with the balance of trade; they change the amount of trade, but the balance is still there. The optimum of foreign trade for any nation is that amount which will occur voluntarily when there are no artificial barriers to trade. It must be kept in mind that the term *trade* as used here refers to all exchanges—including services or travel or money or other types of "invisible" trade, as well as goods. The term refers to *economic* balance, rather than to *physical* balance.

When governments use tariffs and other trade restrictions as instruments to influence, restrain, or coerce other peoples or governments, the field of international politics and intrigue is entered. If history offers any basis for judgment on this subject, it is that sound economics and morality are cast aside at such times. . . .

International politicians seem to assume that trade is a hostile process; that it is a concession granted to friendly nations; and that when it is withheld from unfriendly nations it does harm, without harming the withholder. Even the words sometimes used—*protection, sanction, embargo,* and the like—suggest hostility. They carry the implication of warfare—of doing something to restrain someone.

Actually, trade as engaged in by individuals is generally a friendly exchange. A trader, to be sure, drives the best bargain he can. But when both sides are free to accept or reject offers, the result cannot be hostile to either party. If you're out of gas, you don't feel hostile toward the person who sells you some. . . .

In discussions of foreign trade, the term *most-favored-nation clause* is often used. This clause has, for several decades, been a part of many commercial treaties between nations. Its purpose is to prevent one nation's being treated more favorably than any other nation signing the commercial pact. Thus, no favoritism among the signatory nations. Back of this idea is the concept that by reducing tariffs we are granting a favor to the other nation. We are; but it would be more nearly correct to say that the most favored nation in every such deal is the one granting the reduction. Why is it a sacrificial act to grant a favor in which you yourself will share?

In the great expansion of trade restrictions following World War I, some were imposed with the intent of retaliation. If country A raises a tariff wall against products from the United States, we are hurt by it; there's no doubt about that. Country A, however, may fail to realize that its citizens are hurt to an equal or an even greater degree. So, what do we do about it? We are likely to say: "You can't do this to us!" To drive home our conviction, we raise a retaliatory tariff against the products of country A. And who is affected by it? Country A, to be sure is hurt by our tariff because its people will have greater difficulty in exporting goods to us over the tariff wall; but we, too, are hurt by our tariff against the other country's goods. Our consumers must pay more for imported goods which were formerly brought in duty-free. So the effect of such a combination of tariffs is to impoverish both nations. As Frederic Bastiat put it: "A protective duty is a tax directed against a foreign product; but we must never forget that it falls back on the home consumer."

The view is commonly held that in a world of widespread economic nationalism, where nations have raised tariff walls against nations, our only hope of survival is to do likewise. We must meet tariffs with tariffs—fight fire with fire. Such, of course, is not the case. Even if every single nation in the world raised tariffs against our products, we would gain in at least two ways by leaving our own borders open for the importation of goods. First, as consumers, we would benefit by the importation of goods and services shipped in at costs below those for which we could produce them. Second—and perhaps more important—this gesture would do more to establish friendly relations between nations than any other single thing we might do. Other nations would soon observe the wisdom of such a move and follow our example. . . .

National self-sufficiency is sometimes expressed as "economic nationalism," "isolationism," or the "keep the money at home" idea. The argument is that we would be better off, as a nation, if we did not trade with other nations. We would develop our own resources more fully; we would encourage domestic employment; and we would not become dependent on other nations for goods and services.

On the question of dependency, it should be recalled again that trade is a two-way project. For example, if we gear our industry to the use of imported lead, we are, of course, dependent on foreign production of lead. But the foreign producer is just as dependent on our market for whatever he receives in trade for his lead. It is not a one-way street.

One might as well argue that the automobile worker in Detroit should not be dependent on the farmer for his food, nor the farmer dependent on the Detroit worker for his automobile. The farmer is as dependent on the automobile worker for his market as the automobile worker is dependent on the farmer for food. It is as logical to argue self-sufficiency for an individual as for a nation. As a matter of fact, the type of dependence engendered by free trade between individuals is a wholesome thing. So long as it is voluntary trade, friendships develop. Such trade is not a battle between opposing forces, as is sometimes claimed. Witness the friendships between the customers and the tradespeople in a small community. . . .

Basically, the issue of tariffs and other trade restrictions is a moral one. This is not to deny that it is also an economic issue. It is merely a matter of emphasis. Unless economic principles are in harmony with good moral principles, they are not good economics.

Government grows strong and dictatorial by the granting of special favors. Trade restrictions are just another of the handouts which a government can grant, thereby increasing its power over individuals—to the detriment of all. . . .

The moral basis for free trade rests on the assumption that an individual has the right to the product of his own labor—stealing is bad because ownership is good. This involves property rights. . . . The right to own property involves the right to use it, to keep it, to give it away, or to exchange it. Unless this is possible, one does not own property. To lay obstacles in the path of ownership, use, or exchange of property is a violation of the human right to own property. . . .

It isn't necessary for all nations to agree jointly and simultaneously to remove restrictions. If only one nation does it, some good is accomplished—both for itself and for its customers. A great nation, such as the United States, could do it and thus set an example for others to follow. It would not be meddling in the affairs of other nations; it would merely be looking after the best interests of its own citizens. And instead of being resentful, other nations would be eternally grateful.

W.M. Curtiss (1904-1979) served as executive secretary for The Foundation for Economic Education (FEE) in Irvington, New York. This is an excerpt from his book The Tariff Idea, *published by FEE in 1952. It was reprinted in the January 1991 issue of* Freedom Daily, *published by The Future of Freedom Foundation.*

6

The Immorality of Protectionism

by James Bovard

The tariff is the protection the wolf gave the lamb.
—Rep. James Beck, 1882

Protectionism produces political corruption, economic stagnation, and international conflict. Yet, many people will insist that even though protectionism hinders a nation's ability to feed, clothe, and house itself, the moral gains from protectionism are greater than the economic losses. But what is the moral core of protectionism? What is the ethical basis for fair trade as it is practiced?

Every restriction on imports is an attempt by the U.S. government to compel some Americans to pay higher prices to other Americans than they otherwise would have paid. No consumer offers to voluntarily pay these higher prices: they pay higher prices only because 17,000 U.S. Customs Service officials leave them no choice. Henry George observed over a hundred years ago:

> Protective tariffs are as much applications of force as are blockading squadrons, and their object is the same—to prevent trade. The difference between the two is that blockading squadrons are a means whereby nations seek to prevent their enemies

41

from trading; protective tariffs are a means whereby nations attempt to prevent their own people from trading.

Yale University professor William Graham Sumner noted in the last century: "No coercion is necessary to make men buy dollars at 98 cents apiece. The case for coercion is when it is desired to make them buy dollars at 101 cents apiece." Even when a person does not buy an imported product, the price of the competing domestic product is higher because of the restriction on foreign competition.

Trade barriers raise prices, and price hikes have the same effect as a federal decree that some Americans shall no longer be allowed to buy the restricted product. As John Stuart Mill noted in his essay "On Liberty," "Every increase of price is a prohibition to those whose means do not come up to the augmented price. . . ." Government cannot drive up prices without knocking some people out of the market—without taking a notch out of someone's living standards, changing the types of clothes some people wear, the cars some people drive, the food some people eat, the medical care some people receive. The 1986 Softwood Lumber Agreement added $1,000 to the cost of constructing a new house in the U.S., thereby knocking as many as 300,000 people out of the home-buying market—effectively decreeing that many families would be forced to live in trailer homes (so-called tornado magnets) instead of a real house. If the federal government intervened to cause old people's bones to automatically break when the elderly fall, that would be denounced as the height of idiotic tyranny. But, as long as federal policy consists instead of a quota that imposes the equivalent of a 170 percent tariff on dairy imports, thereby insuring that many Americans will have calcium deficiencies and weak bones, that is okay. What is the moral difference between putting a 50 percent surcharge on imported clothing and commanding millions of poor people to wear tattered garments?

All trade barriers rest upon the moral premise that it is fairer for the U.S. government to effectively force an American citizen to buy from an American company than to allow him to voluntarily make a purchase from a foreign company. U.S. trade policy assumes that the moral difference between an American company and a foreign company is greater than the difference between coercion and voluntary agreement. The choice of fair trade versus free trade is ultimately this: Is coercion ever fairer than voluntary agreement?

Every trade restraint is a moral issue, forcibly sacrificing some Americans for the benefit of other Americans. Treasury Secretary Robert Walker observed in 1845: "If the marshall were sent by the federal government to collect a direct tax from the whole people, to be paid over to the manufacturing capitalists to enable them to sustain their business, or realize a larger profit, it would be the same in effect as the protective duty." If a businessman pulls a gun on a customer and demands 20 percent more for a product, that is robbery. If a politician intervenes to the same effect, it is fair trade.

Protectionism rests upon a moral glorification of an economy's least competitive producers. Senator Ernest Hollings announced in 1988: "The market will take care of consumers. The Government must take care of producers. No government was ever organized to get everybody something for a cheap price. The market does that." (Hollings made this observation in a speech calling for further government suppression of the market.) Protectionists murder the market and then scorn consumers for being orphans.

Fair trade is based on the doctrine that producers have rights and consumers have duties. Fair trade assumes that the consumer's freedom of choice is an injustice to the producer. The soul of protectionism is that if a company cannot stand on its own two feet, government should force its customers to carry it. Protectionism is an economic no-fault insurance policy: no matter how often an American company crashes in the marketplace, the consumer must pay the bill.

Protectionism is a Dred Scot policy for consumers—the federal government promising not to let American consumers escape from American businesses who want to charge them higher prices. Protectionism means shackling some people in order to enrich other people. As Ambrose Bierce observed, a tariff is a "tax on imports designed to protect the domestic producer against the greed of his consumer."

Government cannot restrict trade without redistributing income. Tariffs, as a government tax for private benefit, are either fair or unfair. Either the government has a moral justification for imposing a 7.4 percent surcharge on wooden clothespins imports for the benefit of U.S. clothespin makers—or it does not. U.S. trade policy implicitly assumes that fair trade can be achieved by giving certain officials unlimited power to ordain how many of each foreign good other Americans may buy, and exactly what surcharge they must pay. But the mathematical precision of American tariffs and quotas makes a mockery of any reasonable concept of fairness. If we assume that current trade laws are fair, then if the tariff on orange juice, currently 40 percent, was instead 41 percent, it would be unfair to American consumers; and if it was 39 percent, it would be unfair to

American orange growers. Would allowing Americans to consume more than two foreign peanuts per person per year be unfair to American peanut growers?

Under U.S. law, voluntary agreements between Americans and foreigners are the test of fairness for some products, while for other products, political dictates determine fairness. If a person wants to buy an Italian sweater, he may spend his dollars as he chooses; but if he prefers to buy an identical sweater made in Korea, the U.S. government intervenes by establishing quotas on how many such sweaters Americans can buy. The difference between goat cheese and cow cheese requires antithetical rules of fairness—letting goat cheese imports be determined by unconstrained wheeling and dealing, while cow cheese imports are determined by presidential proclamations establishing import quotas.

Fair trade in practice means a moral and political deification of high prices. American trade law assumes that there are dozens of things that can make an imported product's price unfairly low, but almost nothing that can make an import's price unfairly high. U.S. dumping law assumes that American producers are treated unfairly unless a foreign company charges the highest prices in the world to its American customers. Investigations by both the International Trade Commission and the federal Committee for the Implementation of Textile Agreements presume that it is a bad thing if foreign products are priced lower than American products.

Sen. Jesse Helms in 1990 denounced U.S. textile policy "that gives our market to foreigners." Helms apparently believes that the U.S. Congress should have the right and power to give the market to whom it chooses. To talk of giving the market is, in reality, to talk of giving away the dollars of anyone who must depend on that market. To talk of imports' fair share of the U.S. market means to talk of U.S. producers' fair share of American workers' paychecks. For politicians to allocate market share is to treat consumers like serfs who can be freely traded by their lords.

Protectionism means an automatic partial expropriation of the buyers' dollars. The fundamental question of protectionism is: Who should pay the price of a company's lack of competitiveness? Does every needy company have a right to put a partial lien on its customers' bank accounts? In a nation that has thousands of business bankruptcies each year, who should decide which firms or industries should be politically exempted from the rigors of competition?

American trade policy presumes that an exchange between an American and a foreign citizen is fundamentally morally different than trade between two Americans. The question of the fairness of a company's prices now rests on where imaginary lines on a map happen to be drawn—on some deal cut by long-dead politicians or on how much territory some army conquered a few centuries before. Because Nova Scotia never joined the other British colonies in the 1776-1783 revolution, the Commerce Department judged a Canadian company guilty of dumping groundfish in its sales in Boston. Because Britain and the United States agreed in 1849 that the 49th parallel would be the boundary between the western United States and Canada, the Commerce Department condemned as unfairly priced raspberries from Saskatchewan sold in Seattle. If one company charges different prices in Vancouver, Washington, and Miami, Florida, that is fine. But if another company charges exactly the same different prices in Vancouver, Canada, and Miami, Florida, the U.S. Commerce Department rushes out to collect a few hundred thousand pages of documents to find out what went wrong.

Trade barriers come down to a question of political legitimacy. What gives one person a right to arbitrarily and forcibly reduce another person's living standard? Should election into office automatically give a person the right to dictate the food other people eat, the clothes they wear, and the cars they drive? Does winning a seat in Congress mean that a person—or group of people—can rightfully dictate that each American will be allowed only one teaspoon of foreign ice cream a year and that only one American out of 10,000 will be allowed to buy a Czech wool sweater each year? Protectionism is nothing but politically controlled trade—which means political control of the life of the average citizen.

James Bovard is author of The Fair Trade Fraud, The Farm Fiasco, *and, most recently,* Lost Rights: The Destruction of American Liberty. *His articles have appeared in* The Wall Street Journal, The New York Times, Newsweek, *and* Reader's Digest. *This essay appeared in the September 1994 issue of* Freedom Daily, *published by The Future of Freedom Foundation.*

7

The United States: A Protectionist Nation

by James Bovard

In talking about trade, many politicians rely on the Big Lie—the simple assertion that America is the most open market in the world, and therefore that any criticisms of our existing trade policies for being protectionist is absurd. But, sifting through the details of trade policy can provide insight—and entertainment. One of the best ways to defeat protectionists is to show the dirty little details of how protectionist systems operate.

For instance, agricultural import quotas permit each American citizen to consume the equivalent of only *one teaspoon* of foreign ice cream per year, *two foreign peanuts* per year, *one pound* of imported cheese per year, and *one teaspoon* of imported butter. The U.S. International Trade Commission examined the impact of these quotas on consumers a few years ago, and concluded that the peanut import quota had the equivalent impact of a tariff of up to 90 percent while the cheese import quota had the same impact of tariffs as high as 170 percent. Yet, because few Americans know or understand the existence of dairy import quotas, there is little or no public protest against a 170 percent tax on one of the most nutritious foods Americans can eat.

The U.S. also has import quotas on beef from Australia and Argentina, on butter from Europe, and on cotton from Egypt. No matter how tight the quotas, some farm groups are never satisfied: the

47

Clinton administration recently proposed imposing tariffs of over 100 percent on peanut butter imports from Canada as a means to protect high American peanut prices.

Congress is imposing over 8,000 different taxes on imports via the tariff code. While the average American tariff is now around five percent, some tariffs are in the stratosphere. Low-priced watches are hit with an average tariff of 151.2 percent. Tobacco stems must pay a 458.3 percent tariff. Tariffs on some low-priced shoe imports are 67 percent.

The U.S. Tariff Code looks like it was written to encourage the poor to raise their standard of living. If someone buys an imported plastic school satchel, he pays a 20 percent duty. But if he buys a school satchel made of fancy leather, he pays only a 4.7 percent duty. Footwear with outer soles of rubber or plastic, valued at not over $3 a pair, is tariffed at 48 percent; but if it is valued over $12, the tariff is only 20 percent. Soda lime drinking glasses valued at less than 30 cents carry a 38 percent tariff; if valued over $5, the tariff is only 7.2 percent.

Mink furs are duty free. And with the money a mother saves on her mink, maybe she can afford a polyester sweater for her baby— which carries a 34.6 percent tariff. Lobster is duty free; with the savings, struggling parents may be able to afford infant food preparations, which carry a 17.2 percent tariff. Orange juice carries a 40 percent tariff, but Perrier water pays only 0.8 percent.

Orange juice is cheaper in Canada than in the U.S. largely because the Canadians do not have any orange growers—and thus have no tariff on orange juice imports. The tariff on the highest quality brandy is 1.2 percent—while the tariff on the cheapest, rotgut, brown-paper-bag-quality brandy is 41 percent. Worst of all, the tariff on the cheap cigars is three times higher than the tariff on expensive cigars.

The U.S. Tariff Code looks like a variable value-added tax that was concocted in a lunatic asylum. The tariff on brooms is 42.3 percent, thereby safeguarding dust and dirt; the tariff on flashlights is 25 percent, thereby encouraging people to break their noses in the dark; the tariff on cheap scissors is 23.6 percent, thereby encouraging taxpayers to shred their IRS tax forms with their bare hands instead of cutting them neatly into little squares.

One of the favorite examples of the new protectionists of an industry that needs more protection is the textile industry. Textiles have already been heavily protected for over 200 years, and are today our oldest infant industry. The U.S. imposes import quotas on over three *thousand* different textile and apparel products, including tampons, typing ribbons, tarps, twine, towels, tapestries, and ties. Mexico in 1989 was allowed to ship the U.S. only 35,292 bras per year—not even enough to cup the neighboring city of Brownsville, Texas. U.S. textile trade policy is based on the sage insight that clothes are among the most dangerous objects that a nation can import—thus justifying stricter import controls on socks, night-gowns, and hankies than on pistols, rifles, and deadly chemicals.

Importers have been hammered by constant changes in the rules on classifying textile imports. Customs Service officials worked overtime in late 1989 to protect America against foreign shoestrings. Customs prohibited the import of a shipment of 30,000 tennis shoes from Indonesia because the shoe boxes contained an extra pair of shoelaces. One Customs official decided the extra laces were a clothing product that required a separate quota license for importing, and his decision set a precedent for the entire Customs Service. None of the tennis shoe importers were thinking of the extra laces as anything but part of the tennis shoe, and thus they were caught in their tracks without quotas for shoestrings. (Some new tennis shoes have eyelets for more than one set of laces.) Customs proceeded to establish intricate rules for shoelace imports. In a judicious ruling, the U.S. government announced that an extra pair of shoelaces would be permitted in a box of tennis shoes as long as the extra shoelaces were laced into the shoes and were color-coordinated with the shoes. But Customs warned importers, "We note that where multiple pairs of laces of *like* colors and/or designs are imported . . . a presumption is raised" that the shoelaces are not actually part of the shoe. [Italics in the original.]

The 1989 *Economic Report of the President* concluded that tariffs and quota restrictions produce an average effective tariff charge of over 50 percent for apparel imports. Textile trade restrictions hit poor families far harder than rich families. According to a Consumer Expenditure Survey by the Bureau of Labor Statistics, households with the lowest 20 percent of incomes spend almost four times the percentage of their income on clothing as do households in the highest 20 percent. The U.S. Association of Importers of Textile and Apparel estimates that textile and apparel protection costs the poor 8.8 percent of their disposable income. It is difficult to underestimate the fanaticism of the U.S. textile protectionists. In May of last year, President Clinton announced that the United States was sending U.S. troops to Macedonia to safeguard it from the Serbians. But, a few weeks later, while Macedonia was struggling with a flood of refugees from Bosnia and threats of invasion, the U.S. Commerce Department launched a preemptive attack on a trickle of Macedonian clothes exports. The U.S. Commerce Department slashed the amount of wool suits that Macedonia could ship to the U.S. by over 70 percent—permitting only 80,000 per year. A Commerce Department spokesman told me that the quotas were in response to "rampantly rising imports" from Macedonia—but Macedonia was only supplying three percent of the wool suits bought in American. Perhaps the Clinton administration is planning to post U.S. army troops in Macedonia to serve as advance inspectors for the U.S. Customs Service—to keep a closer count on Macedonian exports.

Unfortunately, the Macedonia decision exemplifies the protectionist tendencies of the Clinton administration. The U.S. has imposed new textile import quotas on over fifteen nations since Clinton took office. One of the most surprising new quotas is the early 1994 quota imposed on silk clothing from China. No U.S. company manufactures silk clothing—we do not have any silkworms in this country, and there is no hope that an industry will be established here anytime in the next couple centuries. But a few officials in Washington feared that imports of high-quality silk blouses might be hurting the sale of low-quality polyester blouses made in the U.S.

Every trade barrier undermines the productivity of capital and labor throughout the economy. A 1979 Treasury Department study estimated that trade barriers routinely cost American consumers eight to ten times as much as they benefit American producers. A 1984 Federal Trade Commission study estimated that tariffs cost the American economy $81.00 for every $1.00 of adjustment costs saved. Restrictions on clothing and textile imports cost consumers $1.00 for each 1 cent of increased earnings of American textile and clothing workers. According to the Institute for International Economics, trade barriers are costing American consumers $70 billion a year—equal to over $1,000 per family.

Fair trade consists largely of the U.S. government devising new ways to protect American consumers against the scourge of low prices. The U.S. government does not penalize foreign companies for charging high prices—only for charging low prices. Imported clothing that is priced lower than U.S. clothing is automatically assumed to threaten to disrupt the U.S. market. Fair trade aims not to safeguard competition, but to enrich American competitors. The most common foreign "unfair trade practice" is producing a better product at a lower price. In a nation with hundreds of federal, state, and local consumer protection agencies, consumers are explicitly denied a role in most trade proceedings of the U.S. International Trade Commission and Commerce Department.

U.S. trade policy has been an unending war against abundance. Do we really need tens of thousands of government bureaucrats working to reduce the living standard and buying power of American citizens? Do we need federal employees counting each arriving handkerchief from the Third World, carefully weighing each keg of incoming cheese, and counting the numbers of shoestrings in each box of imported tennis shoes? There was nothing mentioned in the preamble of the U.S. Constitution about forming "a more perfect Union" in order to prevent Americans from eating foreign ice cream.

The time has come to deregulate our national borders—to end the medieval pursuit of a "just price" for imports—and to cease allowing government officials to have economic life-and-death power over American businesses. It should not be a federal crime to charge low prices to American consumers.

This essay appeared in the October 1994 issue of Freedom Daily, *published by The Future of Freedom Foundation.*

8

U.S. Misfortunes "Made in America"

by Lawrence W. Reed

T wo crucial points need to be made about international trade: 1) The U.S. is far more interventionist than is commonly believed, and 2) our competitiveness problems are primarily made in America, not overseas.

When former president Bush visited Australia a few years ago, Australian farmers staged a very visible protest. They did us Americans a great public service. They pointed out that America's agricultural export subsidies are effectively a form of "dumping"—the very practice our politicians like to rail about when Americans are the supposed "victims." Australian farmers have lost markets because subsidized American grain is stealing away their customers.

The notion that America has wide-open borders and that only nasty foreigners restrict imports is political poppycock—pure disinformation that self-serving special interests and their gullible allies in Washington are more than happy to promote. James Bovard, one of this country's foremost trade experts, notes that Congress has imposed more than 8,000 different taxes on imports, with some as high as 458 percent.

In a December 9, 1991, article in *Newsweek*, Bovard pointed out that U.S. trade law effectively "means permitting each American citizen to consume the equivalent of only one teaspoon of foreign ice cream per year, two foreign peanuts per year and one pound of foreign cheese per year." Furthermore, it is a fact that "Mexico may sell Americans only 35,292 bras a year, that Poland may ship us only 350 tons of alloy tool steel a year, and that Haiti is allowed to sell the United States only 7,730 tons of sugar."

These barriers don't just hurt foreigners; they injure Americans who rely on low-cost imports for their very jobs or who must export less because they can't keep their cost down by purchasing low-priced imports. To quote Bovard again:

> American manufacturers have been forced to grovel before Commerce Department officials for each ton of specialty steel they are allowed to import. Restrictions on steel-crankshaft imports in 1987 hurt diesel-truck engine manufacturers, restrictions on ball-bearing imports in 1989 hurt scores of American industries and restrictions on flat-panel computer displays hurt computer makers in 1991. Thanks to economically perverse U.S. trade laws, the more inefficient and backward an American industry is, the more likely the U.S. government will blame foreign companies for its problems.

Japan has half the population of the U.S., yet some people think it should buy just as much from us as we buy from it. Even so, the average Japanese in 1990 bought $395 worth of American goods, while the average American bought $359 worth of products from Japan. Maybe that's why protectionists never express the balance of trade on a per-capita basis; they prefer to confuse people with raw, almost meaningless numbers.

Another revealing way to look at the picture, according to *The Detroit News*, is in these terms: About 1.7 percent of Japan's GNP went for purchasing American products in 1990, compared with 1.6 percent of our GNP that went toward buying Japanese goods.

Lee Iacocca, shortly before departing with Mr. Bush for Asia, lamented that Americans sold just 15,000 cars to Japan in 1991, while they sold 3.8 million cars to us. But Honduras sold far more bananas to the U.S. than the U.S. sold to Honduras. And surely more soybeans left the U.S. for Denmark than Denmark sent here. If trade is supposed to be car for car, banana for banana, bean for bean, then what's the point?

The cold, hard facts were expressed best by the comic-strip character Pogo years ago: "We have met the enemy and he is us." Why has U.S. competitiveness suffered in recent years? Because our government-monopoly schools have turned out functional illiterates by the millions; our federal government refuses to live within its means and sucks hundreds of billions of dollars from the capital market each year to pay its deficits; our capital gains tax, highest in the industrialized world, is decisively anti-investment; our bureaucracy imposes countless, costly regulations in the name of fuel economy, civil rights, and disabled people; and while Japan strongly encourages savings, we fritter them away with confiscatory taxation.

Clyde Prestowitz of the Economic Strategy Institute has shown that just the Tax Reform Act of 1986 alone jacked up the cost of capital in America by 40 percent. Add to that the fact that our overpaid auto executives still haven't figured out where the steering wheel should be for cars bound for Japan, and you get the picture.

So don't be suckered into bashing the rest of the world for misfortunes that originate here. Such distractions may elect politicians, but they don't solve problems.

Lawrence W. Reed is president of The Mackinac Center for Public Policy in Midland, Michigan. This essay appeared in the April 1994 issue of Freedom Daily, *published by The Future of Freedom Foundation.*

9

What President Clinton Should Have Said to the Japanese

by Jacob G. Hornberger

In 1993, President Clinton visited Japan. The following is a model speech that the president could have delivered to the Japanese people:

I am deeply grateful for the opportunity to visit Japan and to speak to you, the Japanese people, during my first year as president of the United States. I am here not only to fortify friendships between our nations, but also to announce major changes regarding relations between the U.S. and Japan.

For many years, politicians and bureaucrats have believed that trade is a win-lose situation. We have believed that whenever two people enter into an economic exchange, one of them will win from the exchange and the other will lose. Thus, we have always viewed economic activity as a form of warfare between people.

But politicians and bureaucrats have been wrong. Trade between individuals is actually a win-win situation for the people entering into the exchange. A person will exchange something he values less for something he values more. For example, suppose a person owns ten apples and another owns ten oranges. By exchanging one apple for one orange, both of them give up something they value less for something they value more.

Why is this so significant? *Because it shows that people's standards of living can increase through the simple act of trade!* In other words, people can improve their own well-being by entering into exchanges with others. And the corollary of this principle is equally important: *to the extent that any government interferes with people's ability to exchange freely with one another, to that extent the state is interfering with people's pursuit of happiness and their economic well-being.*

Therefore, it is essential that people all over the world have the widest latitude for freely engaging in economic trade.

But I come before you tonight not simply to speak about economic principles. I also wish to do something much more important and profound. I want to make confessions and apologies this evening on behalf of the United States government—to both you and the American people.

Many years ago, governments in the United States began forcing our citizens to send their children to state-approved schools where they would learn only the doctrine which we, the governmental officials, wanted them to learn. And much of the indoctrination that the children received was false.

For example, most Americans honestly believe that they live in a land of "free enterprise." They believe this because they have been taught to believe it in their state-approved schools. If any of you ever visits our nation, simply ask any American about his "free-enterprise" system, and he will bubble over with enthusiasm as he says, "America is a land where you can enter into any enterprise without regulation or restriction; where you can become phenomenally wealthy by freely selling goods and services to others; where you can travel anywhere without restriction; where you can buy and sell without political interference. America is the land of free enterprise."

It is a sad sight. The truth—which more and more Americans are now discovering, despite their many years of government-approved schooling—is that America is not a land of free enterprise—and has not been for some sixty years. The truth is that ours is a welfare state and a regulated economy deceptively termed "free enterprise."

In our land of "free enterprise," the state takes about forty percent of people's income. A large percentage of the money is used to support thousands and thousands of public officials; the rest of the money is given to people who have privileged connections to governmental officials. We require people to seek our permission to do business through licensing and permit requirements. We punish them if they travel to nations whose governments are not friendly to our government. And we do not permit them to trade freely with others.

And I confess to you and the American people that this way of life—the welfare state and the managed economy—is a miserable failure. The welfare state was supposed to end poverty. It did not. Our managed economy was supposed to bring safety and security to the American people. It did not. Taxes continue to rise; regulations continue to increase; the number of governmental officials continues to expand; government spending continues to soar.

The truth is that our economic system is a disaster.

Unfortunately, American governmental officials hate the term "responsibility." None of them has ever done what I am doing tonight—accepting responsibility for what we in the government have done to the American people and their well-being.

What has been the standard response of U.S. governmental officials to America's economic woes? To blame you, the Japanese people, for our difficulties. We constantly refer to the so-called "trade imbalance" between the U.S. and Japan. But hardly ever do we do the same with respect to other nations. We have found it easier to foment anger and resentment against Orientals than against Caucasians.

I confess that you—the Japanese people—are not the cause of our economic difficulties. It was wrong of our governmental officials not to accept responsibility for the failure of our welfare state and managed economy. It was equally wrong of us to appeal to prejudices against Orientals. And it was wrong of us to deceive the American people about the type of economic system under which they lived.

On behalf of the United States government, I apologize to both you and the American people for the grievous wrongs that we governmental officials have committed.

Actually, you—the Japanese people—are part of the economic solution for America. But before explaining how you hold a key to our economic problems, please permit me to go back in history about half-a-century.

During the past fifty years, America's governmental-approved schoolteachers have taught our citizens that for the United States, World War II began with the Japanese attack on Pearl Harbor. On behalf of my government, I publicly confess to you and to the American people that this is false. The truth is that prior to December 7, 1941, the U.S. government, led by President Franklin D. Roosevelt, engaged in several acts of war against your nation.

For example, prior to your nation's attack at Pearl Harbor, American military forces, led by General Claire Chennault, repeatedly attacked Japanese military forces on the mainland of China.

American governmental officials maintained that Chennault's "Flying Tigers" were simply a private force assisting the Chinese to resist your government's aggression. This was false, and our public officials knowingly lied about it. General Chennault's forces were actually U.S. government military forces operating under the guise of a private force, and their operations were funded by our government. These attacks by our military forces against those of your nation occurred prior to your government's attack on Pearl Harbor. And they were expressly authorized by President Roosevelt.

Moreover, by imposing an embargo against Japan on oil and other essential items, our government engaged in what has always been considered an act of war under international law. And the American government seized and confiscated Japanese assets located in the United States, even though a state of war did not exist between our nations.

Why did President Roosevelt engage in this course of action? Prior to Pearl Harbor, the American people strongly opposed entry into the European war. And although President Roosevelt himself stated that he stood with the American people on this issue, there is now no doubt that Roosevelt was not telling the truth—that, in fact, he wanted desperately to involve the U.S. in the conflict. But due to the American people's strong opposition to entering the European conflict, Roosevelt knew that he could never achieve this end unless the Germans attacked the U.S. first. Yet, despite repeated provocations by the United States, the Germans refused to take Roosevelt's bait.

The shameful truth about Roosevelt's actions toward Japan in 1941 is one which our government has never before acknowledged, even though the circumstantial evidence leads irresistibly to but one conclusion: President Roosevelt sought a "back door" to the European war by doing everything he could to provoke your nation into attacking the United States first.

We must ensure that this type of conduct never happens again. To entrust political leaders with powers to control trade and to confiscate assets during peacetime is much too dangerous. For unscrupulous political leaders are too often tempted to use and abuse such powers. It is a slippery slope to real war when one nation wages economic warfare against another. In the words of Frederic Bastiat, the 19th-century, free-trade leader in France, "When goods are not allowed to cross borders, soldiers will."

Therefore, upon my return to Washington, as president of the United States, I am proposing to the United States Congress an amendment to the U.S. Constitution that reads as follows: "Neither the Congress nor the states shall enact any laws respecting the regulation of commerce nor abridging the free exercise thereof."

This amendment will result in the elimination of such political controls as licensing and permit laws, import and export restrictions, and all economic regulations. By separating the economy and the state, we will embark on the road to peace and prosperity.

There are those who say, "The U.S. should not free the American people until the Japanese government frees the Japanese people." But this is false and fallacious. People have a right to be free, regardless of whether others are free or not. Moreover, even if your government prohibits some of you from buying wheat or any other product from American sellers, it would be irrational for our government to prohibit Americans from buying automobiles, steel, and other products from Japanese sellers.

As I have indicated, the more trade, the better. We shall unilaterally drop all trade restrictions, not only because it is the way to economic prosperity, but, more important, because people should be free to do what they want with their own money. Perhaps you—the Japanese people—will be able to enlighten your public officials to do the same.

Part II

At the end of World War II, the United States was the economic leader of the world. Since our geographic territory had not suffered the ravages of war, we led the world in the production of goods and services. A devastated Europe and Japan eagerly accepted American products, not so much because they wanted them but because they needed them. American businessmen believed that their success was predominantly due to their management practices, which they considered "unquestionably superior" to any other.

Americans became complacent. As a result, they failed to listen to the words of people like W. Edwards Deming and Joseph Juran.

Most Americans have never heard of these two men. But the Japanese people have. They, along with such notable Japanese men as Genichi Taguchi and Kaoru Ishikawa, are considered by many to be the people primarily responsible for the Japanese revolution in quality that has taken place in the last thirty years. As you know, your emperor has honored Dr. Deming by awarding the Deming Prize to the company that each year demonstrates the highest standards of quality.

Time prevents me from fully exploring Deming's philosophy of management. But suffice it to say that, unlike other management advisers, Deming did not offer gimmicks or tricks to ensure high standards of quality. In his book, *Out of the Crisis*, Deming sets forth an entirely new and revolutionary approach to management—a perspective that emphasized an understanding of statistical analysis, the concept of variation, the role of worker creativity and joy in work, the destructiveness of employee ratings, the misplaced reliance on mass inspection (by sorting good from bad) to ensure quality, and the importance of cooperation in the workplace.

Unfortunately, Americans refused to listen to Deming. But when he came and lectured in Japan after the war on the invitation of General Douglas MacArthur, Japanese businessmen listened. Deming told them that if they adopted his methods rather than those which the world had been using since the Industrial Revolution, they would soon lead the world in the quality of manufactured goods.

The result has been the Japanese revolution in quality in the manufacture and production of goods and services. Through Deming's methods, the Japanese discovered that quality and high cost were not necessarily synonymous. In fact, they learned how to improve their operations so that improved quality and lower production costs were possible. At one point, the Japanese could produce, ship, and sell cars in America lower than American manufacturers could produce them. The quality was better and the price was less! Japanese products quickly gained market share. And it all began with two Americans in Japan—W. Edwards Deming and Joseph M. Juran!

American businessmen first tried to explain away what happened in Japan with such comments as "Their culture is different." But when Japanese companies successfully maintained the same high standards of quality and lower production costs in their American plants, that argument soon fell by the wayside.

Then, American businessmen ran to our governmental officials exclaiming:

"Please protect us from those horrible Japanese competitors who are making better products than we are. We don't want to change our methods. We want to continue doing things the way we always have. We want Americans (and Japanese!) to be forced to buy our higher-cost goods. Please protect us from those big, bad bullies who are making such high-quality products and dumping them on our markets."

And our government responded by enacting protectionist barriers all around the United States. And every year, the barrier has been built higher and higher to ensure that American businesses can continue to sell their higher-cost and sometimes lower-quality goods to their fellow Americans.

We were wrong to react in this way to the new world of quality that your nation began. As many of you know, Ford, General Motors, IBM, Xerox, Motorola, and hundreds of other firms are now studying and adopting the management principles set forth by Deming, Juran, Taguchi, and Ishikawa. We have a long way to go, but you have shown us the way to ever-improving standards of quality in the production of goods and services. For this, the American people owe Japan and these men a deep debt of gratitude.

Thus, a key to the future success of American business lies not in prohibiting Americans from purchasing Japan's high-quality goods and not in forcing Japanese to purchase America's higher-cost goods. Instead, the future for American business lies in following the lead of Japan in the area of managing for quality.

But it is necessary to go one major step further.

As I indicated earlier, America's welfare state and managed economy have failed miserably in improving the economic well-being of the American people. Unfortunately, many public officials are looking to quality-management principles as a last-gasp effort to save this failed way of life. They want to "reinvent government." These governmental officials believe that a "more efficient" government is the answer to America's woes. Bureaucrats in the IRS, Department of Defense, Navy, Air Force, and numerous other agencies are endeavoring to adopt Deming's philosophy in order to streamline their operations. I confess that I, too, recognized the benefits of Deming's philosophy and pushed for total quality management for government. But I am afraid that my hopes were misguided and misplaced. Let me explain.

As the brilliant economist Ludwig von Mises pointed out, in an unhampered market economy, the consumer is king. By his buying and abstention from buying, he guides the businessmen's decisions as to which goods and services to produce. If the businessman fails to provide a product which consumers desire, the consumers will go elsewhere. Thus, capital is constantly allocated and reallocated in the marketplace according to the demands and wishes of the consumers.

Dr. Deming affirms the importance of the consumer in his philosophy of management. He says that management must reorient itself to focus constantly on each customer in the production process—not only the ultimate customer but "customers" within the firm, as well.

Both Mises and Deming emphasize the major guiding principle of the unhampered market economy and the private firm: *the element of voluntarism that characterizes the entire process*. At no time can the

63

producer force the consumer to purchase his goods or services. He must produce the quality of product that the consumer *voluntarily* wishes to purchase. Thus, the consumer remains the sovereign. If a firm continually fails to satisfy the consumer, it fails to make a profit and ultimately goes out of business.

The state operates on entirely different principles. It relies not on voluntarism but on force. Behind every governmental rule, regulation, prohibition, and tax are the state's constabularies, jails, and fines. What guides the state are not prices in the marketplace— and not profits resulting from consumer satisfaction—but rather strict obedience to the rules and regulations of the state. When dealing with the state, the "consumer" must either obey or be punished.

Therefore, Deming's principles of management cannot be used to save America's welfare state and managed economy. For consumer sovereignty to prevail, the consumer must be free to say "no" without the threat of punishment.

More fundamentally, the last thing that Americans need are well-oiled, finely tuned governmental bureaucracies more efficiently plundering their fortunes and interfering with their lives.

There is another important point that needs to be made about America's welfare state.

The American people have lost faith and confidence in themselves. They are scared of competition not only from you—the Japanese people—but also from Mexicans, Canadians, Germans, and others from around the world. There is only one way to recapture the strong sense of self-confidence, self-reliance, and self-esteem that were once hallmarks of the American people: to end, not reform, America's welfare-state way of life.

The American people have become too dependent on the state for their well-being. And this has meant a tremendous increase in governmental power in the last fifty years. Ironically, however, a strong government has resulted in a weak people. It saddens Hillary and me when we hear my fellow Americans exclaim, "How would we survive without Social Security, welfare, subsidies, food stamps, and grants?" A once-proud people now cringe in fear at the thought of losing their dole.

Some consider it cruel when the mother bird throws her young out of the nest, but it is not. It is a law of nature—the bird will fly and soar when it must.

While many will consider this to be cruel, it is high time to throw the American people out of their welfare-state nest. *It is time to end, not reform, America's governmental dole*. It is time for the American

64

people to regain the sense of pride and self-confidence that characterized their ancestors.

Therefore, upon my return to Washington, as president of the United States, I am proposing the following amendment to our Constitution: "Neither the Congress nor the states shall have the power to grant any subsidy, welfare, or other special privilege to anyone, regardless of race, class, creed, or economic status." I want to throw the American people out of their governmental nest and see them soar as eagles!

All of my life, I have believed in and supported the socialist notion of the welfare state and the managed economy. Thus, some of you are probably wondering how I have come to these dramatically different views about the role of the state in economic affairs. For this, I shall be eternally grateful to my beautiful wife, Hillary. Every night for the past several months, she has been making me read the works of Frederic Bastiat, Ludwig von Mises, Leonard Read, Friedrich Hayek, Henry Hazlitt, Milton Friedman, Ayn Rand, and many other free-market thinkers. Hillary has shown me the way—the way to freedom for the American people, the way to peace in the world, the way to prosperity and harmony for all.

Prior to my election, I called for major change. Now it is time to enact it.

Well, I suppose I have been rather long-winded tonight, which, as many of my political opponents in America will tell you, is nothing new for me. But I believed that my message of friendship and freedom was so important that you would forgive my lengthy address.

The American people extend their arms in friendship. We have much to learn from you, and perhaps we can be of much assistance to you. Thank you for the courtesy and hospitality that you have shown to Hillary and me. Good night.

This essay appeared in the October 1993 and December 1993 issues of Freedom Daily, *published by The Future of Freedom Foundation.*

10

The Forgotten Argument for Free Trade

by Samuel Bostaph

Like most public policy debates in the United States of the Bush-Clinton era, the debates preceding congressional approval of the North American Free Trade Agreement (NAFTA) consisted mostly of extensive public wrangling over who might gain and who might lose if NAFTA passed.

Self-proclaimed champions for various special-interest groups debated the job-creating versus job-destroying potential of the agreement, the implications of the continuing U.S. export surplus with Mexico for U.S. and Mexican business interests, and the possible results of freer trade for Mexican and U.S. economic development in the future.

Meanwhile, the main argument for free trade got lost in the public arena shuffle. The same is true of the current debate concerning the General Agreement on Tariffs and Trade (GATT). There is as yet no evidence that issues lying deeper than those seemingly related to national advantage or disadvantage will be discussed.

The reason for this may be that the basic argument for free trade identifies no guilty winners or innocent losers *in principle* and so lacks the political ingredient that modern politicians need for plying their real trade—selling spurious cures for imaginary ailments in the body politic. It also may be that arguments about principles are necessarily a rare breed in a society increasingly committed to the ethics of plunder, rather than to those that enable the creation of wealth.

In any event, in principle and very briefly put, the main economic argument for the benefits of free trade is that it stimulates persons, cities, regions, and countries to specialize in the commodities in which they are the relatively most efficient producers. It does so by introducing the element of foreign competition into domestic markets, thus forcing existing domestic producers either to match the quality and productive efficiency of foreign producers or to move their assets into other (more productive) areas.

Whether foreign or domestic, competition is always the attempt to lower costs and prices through greater productive efficiency. And greater productive efficiency is rewarded with greater outputs and expanded markets. Under free trade, the domestic population is able to enjoy a higher standard of living by trading part of their now greater domestic production for the different commodities produced elsewhere.

Just as we would each be poorer if we each tried to be completely self-sufficient, so we would be poorer if we put walls around our cities, our states, or all the United States in the attempt to create self-sufficient local, state, or national economies. Self-sufficiency and the standard of living are inversely related in a civilized world. In choosing between a lower and a higher standard of living, why deliberately choose the lower?

Concerning the question of winners and losers, and contrary to what many have said in the free-trade debates, free trade does not necessarily create more jobs. True, this may happen if unemployment exists and industries stimulated by free trade expand. But even if everyone were fully employed to begin with, producers in a country that opens its borders to free trade will be stimulated by import competition to increase the output of those commodities in which they are relatively more efficient, i.e., have lower production costs relative to foreign producers.

This does mean job losses in high-cost industries and job gains in low-cost industries. It also means an increase in the standard of living for the whole population as prices of consumer goods drop. Without government policies that subsidize or encourage unemployment, net job growth must match labor force growth.

The alternative is to protect relatively high-cost industries against import competition to "preserve the jobs" of those who work in them, and thus force consumers to accept a lower general standard of living. This is what some opponents of free trade—notably, labor unions and those who curry their favor—are really asking.

It also certainly is not the purpose of free trade to make possible export surpluses. Common sense should tell everyone that there is no real advantage to sending more products or more value out of a country than are imported into it. The net result for domestic consumers is fewer commodities, i.e., a lower standard of living. After all, exports are what pay for imports.

Under free trade, increased domestic employment in the relatively efficient industries stimulates increased exports and generates the means to purchase the increased imports that contribute to the resultant higher standard of living. An export surplus serves no purpose.

Finally, although free trade contributes to economic development, it does so mainly because of the stimulus to the discovery and exploitation of relative efficiency. Economic development and growth require a great deal more than free trade across borders for their nurture—especially if the foreign sector of the economy is relatively small in comparison to the size of the economy as a whole.

Indeed, economic development and growth are greatest when all market participants may freely trade, not just those on different sides of national borders. The reason for this is simple. The free trade argument is not really an argument concerning trade between people on different sides of borders at all. It applies to all trade. In essence, it says that men who are free to do so will discover their relative production efficiencies and will exploit them to mutual advantage—if they specialize and trade with one another. The resulting higher overall output and living standards cannot be increased by placing barriers between traders, they only can be diminished. And this effect is the same whether the barrier is placed at some political border or takes the form of a purely domestic trade restriction. In this sense, in the absence of free trade for everyone, we are all losers.

Samuel Bostaph *is the head of the economics department at the University of Dallas in Irving, Texas. This essay appeared in the October 1994 issue of* Freedom Daily, *published by The Future of Freedom Foundation.*

11

The Ghost of Protectionism Past: The Return of Friedrich List

by Richard M. Ebeling

T he cover of the December 1993 issue of *The Atlantic Monthly* had a caricature of Adam Smith running away while being chased by a rain of rotten apples, stones, and copies of a book with the name Friedrich List on their covers. The caption under the drawing said, "Move over Adam Smith. Some of the world's strongest economies run on a different philosophy, and the United States had better take heed." Inside, author James Fallows proceeded to explain "How the World Works."

Mr. Fallows argued that the world economy does not work on the basis of the principles of free trade. Rather, all countries, great and small, operate their international economic relationships on the basis of managed trade. And if America is to match its competitors and be a winner in the global game of commerce and exchange, the United States should do the same. The guide for winning this game, we were told, is Friedrich List.

In the early 1820s, Friedrich List, a German journalist and former professor of political economy, came to America to avoid imprisonment for having criticized the government of the German principality of Württemberg. He took up farming near Harrisburg, Pennsylvania, and edited a German-language newspaper. Having arrived in the United States with letters of introduction from General Lafayette, he soon developed friendships with President Andrew Jackson, Henry Clay and James Madison. List returned to Germany in 1832 as American consul to the city of Hamburg. In 1841, he published a book entitled *The National System of Political Economy*. In 1846, while suffering from a painful and terminal illness, List committed suicide at the age of 57.

What was so special about this man? Friedrich List's significance is that his book became one of the most important rationales for protectionism and government intervention during the remainder of the 19th century. Indeed, his arguments—and the arguments of those whom he inspired—were the basis for the rejection of free trade and for the revival of protectionism and interventionism in Imperial Germany during the second half of the last century.

Three premises were at the foundation of List's protectionist system. First, the idea of "the infant industry." List argued that a country entering the early stages of industrialization was at a disadvantage in relation to those nations that were already industrialized. The new, industrializing firms could not successfully compete against the established foreign industrial enterprises that had already incurred all the required start-up costs and that could sell their products at prices that reflected all the cost-efficiencies of mass production and an already existing highly skilled labor force. The government of an industrializing nation had to erect protectionist barriers to keep the prices of foreign manufactured goods as high as the costs of production of the new industrializing domestic enterprises. Only in this way would those domestic firms have a chance to survive in the market and establish themselves firmly enough to finally face the older foreign industrial enterprises on an open field of free trade at some point in the future.

Second, the idea of "forced capital investment." List said that a nation that specialized in those lines of production dictated by the profitable opportunities offered by international commerce under free trade could find itself locked into low-income-earning activities, escape from which might be impossible. In his eyes, a nation that specialized primarily in agriculture or the selling of raw materials on the world market would never have the same income-earning capacity as those nations specializing in capital-intensive manufacturing. Thus, while protectionism might impose higher short-term costs on a nation's consumers, in the long run, the manufacturing enterprises that were nurtured behind protectionist barriers would enable an industrializing country to have greater productive capability and create a higher standard of living for the people of that nation in the future. And these longer-term benefits would outweigh the short-term losses from paying higher prices for foreign and domestic consumer goods.

Third, the idea of "the national interest." List accused Adam Smith and other free-trade economists of "cosmopolitanism." Men were not a part of a global community, List argued, in which their interests harmonized in a network of international commerce and division of labor. Between man and humanity was the nation, List insisted. Each nation had its own history, culture, stage of development and position of power relative to other nations in the world. And the economic prosperity of each man was tied up with the success or failure of his own nation's struggle for political and economic influence and control in the global competition between nation-states. This meant that for the nation's prosperity and betterment, it was often necessary for the individual to sacrifice his private interest in the arena of trade and profit opportunities for the national interest of the country to which he belonged. Since other nation-states, in the real world, used political power to gain economic advantages for themselves in international trade, one's own nation had to do the same; and to further that end, one's own government had the right and responsibility to regulate and control the economic relations between its citizens and the peoples of other countries.

In his article in *The Atlantic Monthly*, Mr. Fallows insisted that it is the policies of Friedrich List that should explicitly replace the free-trade philosophy of Adam Smith in United States' international economic relations. In fact, Friedrich List—the ghost of protectionism past—has been haunting the world throughout the last hundred years. His ideas and policies have inspired every proponent of state intervention in economic affairs, whether or not they have been aware of the spiritual ancestry of their ideas.

And since the 19th century, the advocates of economic liberty have found it necessary to try to exorcise his spirit from the political body. In 1899, for example, English economist Charles Bastable tried in his book *The Commerce of Nations*. Responding to List's argument for the protection of infant industries and forced capital investment in manufacturing industries, Bastable explained:

> The onus of proof rests with those who advocate [protectionism], and they are bound to show (1) that the industry to be favored will after a time be self-supporting, and (2) that the ultimate advantage will exceed the losses incurred during the process. A careful computation of the different elements involved—the loss in each year of protection, with interest on the

losses during earlier years, the estimated amount of gain to accrue when time for independence [from protection] is reached—will, it appears, tend to the belief that protection as an agent for establishing new and profitable industries is not likely to prove satisfactory. When it is added that the complex and elaborate estimates, which are necessary for a right decision, will have to be made by a legislative body liable to be affected by the influence of interested producers, and at best imperfectly equipped for the task, the risk of trying to encourage by means of protection ought to be sufficiently clear. . . .

The free trade case . . . rests on the broad and well-established fact that the guidance of individual self-interest is, in purely industrial matters, much safer than the direction of even the best-informed Government. . . . All attainable evidence goes to show that where the ordinary conditions of social life are maintained, the care and interest of those concerned in the work of production are by far the best guarantees, for a beneficial employment of the productive resources available. That part of the argument which claims that the power of production is increased by protection . . . rests on the inadmissible assumption that the interest of the producers will not lead them to take up those industries in which productive power will increase most rapidly. The acquisition of industrial skill is quite as likely to advance under free-trade as under protection, though the lines which it takes will probably differ.

And as for the idea that "the national interest" must take precedent over individual, private interests for purposes of peace and prosperity, the Swiss economist William Rappard demonstrated in his 1936 Richard Cobden Lecture, "The Common Menace of Economic and Military Armaments," that this is a policy that leads nowhere but to international conflict and political combat. "By economic armaments," Rappard explained:

[W]e mean all those legislative and administrative devices intended to restrict imports and develop domestic production with a view of reducing international interdependence. Economic armaments are the tools of economic nationalism. . . . The primary source of economic and military armaments . . . we perceive in the doctrine of political nationalism. Political nationalism is the creed which places the national State at the top of the scale of human values, not only above the individual, but mankind itself. It is the creed which . . . leads nations to look

74

upon their own State as a universe in itself and therefore to disregard the rights of all others.

"Economic and military armaments . . . have one common ancestor," Rappard said. "That common ancestor is war. . . . Economic armaments, if persisted in, can make States less interdependent, still less prosperous, and still more antagonistic to each other." Why? Because, "both military and economic armaments, when developed in one State, naturally lead to their development in all the neighboring States."

"That dogmatic, aggressive and defiant [economic] nationalism should have given rise to international tension," Rappard continued, "is shown by the professed ideals of its principal champions." As a demonstration, he quoted from List's *The National System of Political Economy*, in which List stated:

> [A] war which promotes the transition from the purely agricultural to the mixed agricultural-manufacturing state is therefore a blessing for a nation. . . . Whereas a peace, which throws back into a purely agricultural condition a state destined to become industrialized, is a curse incomparably more harmful than a war.

If confronted with the response that his proposal for the conscious implementation of the ideology of Friedrich List may lead to war and greater international tension and conflict, James Fallows would probably reply that such a result is no part of his intentions. But ideologies and policies when consistently and persistently carried out contain within them their own logic and necessary conclusions.

A world in which one nation after another undertook to carry out the Listian ideal would be a world in which those various nations would sooner or later confront each other in their respective desires for domination of various state-supported and subsidized lines of manufacturing, "high-tech" production and service industries in the global market. And in the political battle for global market shares from production and the creation of types of employment preferred over others for their national work forces by governments, either one nation-state concedes and surrenders to the wishes and power of another nation-state or else economic and political warfare must determine the outcome.

Thus, while Mr. Fallows believes that he is being the "realist" in telling the American people about "how the world works," in fact, for that world actually to work in a way leading to greater peace and prosperity, we must, once and for all, renounce the ideas and ideals of Friedrich List. Or as William Rappard expressed it towards the end of his 1936 lecture, "[T]he only hope of humanity therefore lies in a return to the Cobdenite ideals of individual freedom within each nation, and of economic cooperation, peace and goodwill among all nations."

This essay appeared in the April 1994 issue of Freedom Daily, *published by The Future of Freedom Foundation.*

12

The Sanctity of
Private Property

by Jacob G. Hornberger

One of the favorite pastimes of Americans is to look down their noses at the socialist systems which are now crumbling all over the world. Americans honestly believe that the American system of "free enterprise" has prevailed in the battle of "capitalism" versus socialism; and they believe that the world should now simply copy the "private property" system of the American people.

But what is it about the socialist countries which Americans find so objectionable? After all, the socialist nations embody much of that which Americans would never consider abandoning in the U.S.: subsidized housing and medical care for the poor, the prohibition of private citizens from gaining significantly high amounts of wealth, free schooling for all children, and subsidized food for everyone.

But one of the most significant characteristics of the socialist systems is government control over a citizen's ability to sell goods and services to people in other parts of the world. In other words, the essence of the socialist societies in regard to international trade is that the government reigns supreme over the individual and his property; that is, all property in the nation, even when legal title is nominally held in the name of private citizens, is either owned or controlled by the political authorities.

One of the best examples of this lies ninety miles away from American shores. In Cuba, a nation guided by the principles of free public housing, free medical care, free public schooling, and subsidized food for the populace, people are not permitted to sell goods and services to others around the world without the permission of their government officials. The government takes the position that all property ultimately belongs to "the people" and, therefore, subject to political control.

Americans rightfully object to the Cuban way of life. But they have a terrible time recognizing that these same principles are found in 20th-century America. Like his Cuban counterpart, no American is free to sell, without the permission of his public officials, what supposedly belongs to him to people around the world. If an American, for example, decides to sell a quantity of wheat or penicillin to the Cuban people, he is prohibited from doing so by his own politicians and bureaucrats. And Americans are discouraged from traveling to Cuba by an American law that criminalizes the spending of dollars there. This was exemplified last year when an American fisherman was actually sent to jail by *American authorities* for organizing a fishing trip to Cuba.

Now, the American government officials justify this prohibition on the basis that the Cuban ruler, Fidel Castro, is a bad communist (as compared to the apparently "good" communists of Red China, with whom Americans are permitted to trade). But the problem lies not with the American government's determination of who are good communists and who are bad ones. The problem lies with the American people permitting their politicians and bureaucrats to assume and exercise the same power over their lives and property as that found in such nations as Cuba and China.

And despite the fact that the American government maintains ultimate control over the buying and selling decisions of the American people, Americans continue to believe that when American government officials have this control, it is a private property system; and that only when Cuban, Chinese, or Soviet government officials have it, is it considered a socialist system.

What would be a true private property system? One in which the individual is free to buy and sell goods and services anywhere in the world without the interference of his public officials. And it would be a way of life in which people were trading not because the politicians and bureaucrats *permitted* them to do so but rather because they have the *absolute right* to sell whatever belongs to them to anyone anywhere in the world.

78

A second example of this myth of private property in America: oil and gas. Despite their commitment to "free enterprise" and "private property," the American people believe that whenever a person owns what other Americans need, the politicians and bureaucrats must take control over it and redistribute it to the needy.

The best illustration of this tendency toward the socialist principle of public ownership or control over the means of production concerns oil and gas. Whenever the owner of oil or gas decides to sell his product at a higher price than that which American consumers decide is "reasonable," the politicians and bureaucrats, as a result of political pressure from the American people, threaten not only to prohibit him, through price controls, from doing so, but also to take away, through a windfall profits tax, whatever "unjust" profits the producer has made. In other words, while proclaiming the superiority of the American "free enterprise" system over socialist systems in which governments maintain extensive controls over prices and profits, the American people approve of these same socialist principles in their own nation. But, of course, they do so under the rubric of the American "private property" system rather than under the American "socialist" system.

One of the ironies is that during depressed economic conditions, when some oil companies go broke or bankrupt, the American people take the attitude: "That's their problem. They chose to go into the oil business, and they can't cry when it fails to pan out." But when conditions change, and demand for the product suddenly increases, Americans take the same attitude as their counterparts in China, the Soviet Union, and Cuba: "It's not fair for others to have more when I have less. I need the oil and gas. He's gouging me. I am 'forced' to pay these high prices. Take his product and his income away from him and give it to me."

And another irony is that when price controls are instituted, the problems which arise from those controls are never blamed on the controls themselves. Instead, just as in other socialist countries, the problems are always blamed on others, usually "the evil, greedy, profit-seeking, bourgeois swine of a capitalist pig."

The best example of this was the price controls imposed on the oil industry by the American government in the 1970s. What was the result of those controls? The same result found in the Soviet Union, China, and Cuba when price controls are imposed there: shortages and long lines. But did the American people blame them on the political controls themselves? Of course not. That would have been considered unpatriotic. So, the shortages and long lines were blamed on American oil producers. And how do Americans explain the fact that no shortages and long lines have developed as a result of the recent Middle East crisis? They are unable to do so because they have no idea that *only* political control over prices, and not private owners and producers of oil and gas, create shortages and long lines.

The major disaster of price controls and windfall profits taxes, of course, is the abandonment of the sanctity of private property. But the secondary disaster is that the economic situation always becomes worse as a result of the political intervention. People do not realize that prices are simply the market's method of providing signals in the same way that a thermometer uses temperature to provide signals. High prices are simply the market's way of telling people to produce more and consume less. But rather than permit the signals to guide the actions of producers and consumers, the American people pressure their rulers to break the thermometer. Rather than cope with the bad news which the messenger has brought, people instead choose to kill him. And the inevitable result is just like that found in socialist countries everywhere: shortages, long lines, and general market chaos.

When will private property truly be sanctified not only in the U.S. but in other nations as well? Only when the time comes when people stop believing that they have a right to take away what belongs to someone else. There are fewer more destructive forces than the belief that it is acceptable to covet and steal that which belongs to another as long as it is done through the political process. Whether it involves a person's income, his occupational pursuits, his goods and services, or his trading decisions, the succumbing to the urge to take from those who have more will always result in the impoverishment or destruction of the people of a nation regardless of whether they are Romans, British, Soviet, Chinese, Cubans, and, yes, even Americans. As our American ancestors understood so well, only those nations which have a political system which protects free economic activity are those nations in which the citizenry are blessed with peace, prosperity, and harmony.

This essay appeared in the January 1991 issue of Freedom Daily, *published by The Future of Freedom Foundation.*

13

Trade and Immigration Controls Assault the Right to Life

by Sheldon Richman

Ask Americans if they believe in the right to life, liberty, and the pursuit of happiness, and they will say yes. But ask if they believe people should be allowed to buy all the imported products they wish without tariffs or other restrictions, and they will say no. Ask if citizens of other countries should be free to move to the United States without having to get permission from the U.S. government, and—again—they will say no.

How can those positions be reconciled? After all, freedom means the right to take any action that does not entail the use of initiatory force (or fraud). That is the notion of freedom that inspired America's revolutionary generation, and although that vision was not carried out with consistency, in many ways modern America measures up much worse.

Let's look at free trade and free immigration from the perspective of life, liberty, and the pursuit of happiness.

Under free trade, people living in different countries may buy and sell products and services as they wish. Buyers are not penalized with a special tax, a tariff, that only applies to imports. Sellers are not limited by quota to a prescribed number of units. Neither are sellers penalized for "dumping" if they charge "too low" a price in the eyes

81

of the government or domestic competitors. The prices and quantities of imports and exports are left to the free decisions of buyers and sellers, which is to say, the marketplace. When a buyer in Country A and a seller in Country B strike a deal, no one else's rights and freedom are infringed. True, if a buyer purchases an import, he may not buy a similar product from a domestic manufacturer. But that manufacturer is no less free under those circumstances. He has no right to guaranteed sales. He has a right only to offer his products and to deal with consenting buyers. His freedom under free trade is as complete as it could be. (A subsidy in the exporting nation, however objectionable, does not restrict the freedom of competitors in the importing nation.)

However, in a regime of trade restrictions, the would-be buyer of an import is less than free than he would otherwise be. His freedom to buy from whomever he wishes has been blocked. He is forbidden to act on his best judgment with respect to the products he wants to acquire. That restriction is enacted as a favor to someone else. Thus, the buyer's interests are forcibly sacrificed to the manufacturer who refuses to take his chances in the free market.

The advocates of trade restrictions, or protectionism, argue that the buying activities of individuals can harm others. A commercial frequently shown on television has a mother explaining to a child that his father lost his job in the apparel industry because people are buying imports. "Why do they buy that stuff?" the child asks. "I don't know," says the distraught mother as she packs the family's belongings. It is possible that if enough people buy the imported version of a product, the workers making the domestic version could lose their jobs. (Although that is not what has happened in the apparel industry, where technology, not imports, has eliminated jobs.) But that is far from the end of the story, as the commercial implies. The buyers chose imports because they preferred the quality or price or both. If, for higher quality, they paid the same price as, or more than, what was charged for the domestic product, they have enhanced their standard of living. If they paid less, they had money left over, which also enhanced their standard of living. The extra money lets the buyers purchase other products or increase the savings available for investment in new products. Thus, the buyers of imports benefit not only themselves but others also. Who? Those who make the other products they buy with the money saved or those who will benefit from the new investment. Moreover, foreign sellers have acquired dollars, which they will use either to buy American-made products or to invest in the United States. (If they trade them on the world exchange market, the recipients will face the same alternatives.)

The upshot, then, is that those who buy imports may cause some people's jobs to be eliminated, but they also cause other jobs to be created or to pay better. Why should government policy favor the apparel worker over, say, the software programmer?

The free movement of people also meets the test of individual liberty. There is nothing inherently coercive about a foreigner's move to the United States. He pays for transportation. He rents or buys living quarters. He works for a consenting employer or starts his own business. Opponents of free immigration see three complications. First, they argue that immigrants take jobs from Americans or lower wages. Second, they say immigrants consume more in government services than they pay in taxes. Third, they argue that large numbers of immigrants harm everyone else through environmental degradation and crowdedness. Let's take these in turn.

Regarding jobs, the truth is similar to what happens with foreign trade. Immigrants compete for jobs, and that competition may lower wages in selected occupations. But no one's rights are violated by job competition. Further, immigrants create jobs by demanding products and services and by starting businesses. The number of jobs in a free economy is not fixed. There is no reason to fixate on the jobs lost and neglect the jobs gained.

Regarding consumption of government services, Julian Simon and others say that, in fact, immigrants pay more in taxes than they get in services. But even were that not so, the fault would not lie with the immigrants. It lies with the legislators who pass laws providing taxpayer largess to immigrants (and citizens). The simple answer is to stop providing that largess. Those who say that we cannot have free immigration as long as the welfare state exists miss the point. Free immigration will create pressure to cut back, and then eliminate, the welfare state. Its absurdity will be so palpable that people will change their minds about its legitimacy. On the other hand, postponing freedom until the welfare state disappears is self-defeating. How will we get rid of the welfare state if it is saved from its inevitable dislocations and contradictions?

Finally, regarding the environment: This is a variation of the overpopulation argument. It is not the addition of people that creates unhealthy conditions. It is the lack of property rights in resources. If resources are privately owned, entrepreneurs and inventors will have a strong incentive to find the technological solutions to pollution problems. Even the fear of crowdedness through immigration is unfounded. The United States is less densely populated than other industrialized countries. There's plenty of room. The densely populated countries of the West are very wealthy. Western Europe is more densely populated than Africa, Latin America, and China. There is no connection between crowdedness (a highly subjective matter; people often pay a premium to live in densely populated areas) and poverty.

Free trade and free immigration are terms that identify two aspects of personal freedom. Someone who is free need not have permission from the government to buy and sell from any consenting person in the world, and he need not have permission from government to move to another region of the world. The people who say they believe in freedom but who reject free trade and free immigration mistakenly believe that those freedoms are not entailed in the general notion of freedom and that they would violate the freedom of others. We have shown that those arguments are in error.

Freedom is indivisible because the lives of human beings are, in an important sense, indivisible. To live well, a person must be able to plan and act with reference to all aspects of his life throughout his life span. The world is open-ended; one cannot know exactly what one will know tomorrow. Part of the value of freedom is that it gives people the flexibility to grapple with uncertainty. If the government interferes with decisions about from whom one buys products or where one moves, it interferes fundamentally with how people may plan and live their lives. Trade and immigration controls are thus pernicious infringements on the right to life, liberty, and the pursuit of happiness.

Sheldon Richman is senior editor at the Cato Institute in Washington, D.C., and the author of Separating School & State: How to Liberate America's Families, *published by The Future of Freedom Foundation. This essay appeared in the September 1994 issue of* Freedom Daily, *published by The Future of Freedom Foundation.*

14

The Case for
Open Immigration

by Richard M. Ebeling

Not long after the Declaration of Independence was signed in 1776, Thomas Jefferson wrote of "the natural right which all men have of relinquishing the country in which birth or other accident may have thrown them, and seeking subsistence and happiness wheresoever they may be able, and hope to find them."

For most of America's history, our country's door was open to many of those desiring to breathe free and find happiness. Between 1840 and 1940, almost 40 million people came ashore and began a new life. In 1900, 10 million people of foreign birth resided in the United States. Out of a total population of 76 million at the turn of the century, 26 million were the children of foreign-born parents. During the period 1900-1920, another 13.5 million people found a new home and a new beginning in the United States. And between 1931 and 1945, 900,000 more found a haven in America.

This multitude of humanity was not the product of any one culture, but rather of many. In vast numbers, the immigrants came from Britain, Ireland, Germany, Italy, Eastern Europe, the Balkans, Russia, Mexico and various parts of Asia. America was not the child of one racial or cultural strain, but the offspring of many.

In the middle of the 19th century, large numbers of Irish came across the Atlantic to escape famine. In the 1860s and 1870s, many Germans came to escape military conscription in Bismarck's Prussia.

The Chinese arrived to build railroads, sending most of their wages back to China to help family and relatives who faced starvation, and to purchase a plot of land in their native village so that their earthly remains could eventually be buried with their ancestors. The Jews of Poland and Russia came to escape religious persecution and pogroms.

Like a flood, these millions descended upon the coastal cities and then, over time, dispersed across the immense American continent. They began the plowing of the prairies and the building of new towns and cities. Life was often difficult, and many failures and disappointments were faced along the way. But still they came. And they endured. Because even when they discovered that America's cities were not paved with gold, they knew that life was better—and freer—in their new home. And even when their own lot was not one of perfect tranquillity and prosperity, they were confident that their children's lives would be—compared to everything they had left behind in the old country.

In the 1970s, we saw a similar wave of migration to the United States. Our television screens were filled with thousands of Vietnamese boat people who faced drowning, starvation, and attacks by pirates in order to escape from the Communist regime in Hanoi. And we also witnessed their rise from literal rags to increasing riches as they made a new life for themselves and their children in America in a matter of a few years.

And we may soon witness another mass exodus—this time from the Soviet Union. The Soviet government has said that it will issue passports to anyone who desires to leave. The estimates of the number who will want to escape from the collapsing Soviet slave state run from 2 million to 8 million.

Generally, Americans take pride in viewing their country as the melting pot of the world and as the refuge for those escaping from political tyranny and economic disadvantage. But they also often express fear with the arrival of new waves of immigrants. *These fears are totally unfounded. People are America's greatest strength and the source of its continuing prosperity.* Let's examine some of these fears.

1. *Immigrants steal jobs away from Americans.* The premise behind this concern is that there is only a finite amount of work to be done in the American economy and, therefore, a finite number of jobs to be filled. If an immigrant gains employment, therefore, he does so only by displacing an American who previously held that job.

But there is always more work to be done as long as scarcity exists. The ability to supply the various goods and services consumers desire to purchase is limited by the available supply of resources with which those goods and services are produced. Increase the supply of resources at the disposal of the market and the supply of finished goods and services can also be increased.

Immigrants, therefore, rather than stealing away jobs, in fact enable the market to fill jobs for which the labor supply was previously too small. *All* in the society tend to benefit as the general standard of living goes up through the increased quantity and improved quality of all of the marketable goods for which there is a demand.

2. Immigrant labor causes wages to go down and thereby lowers the standard of living of Americans. The way sellers often make their product more attractive to buyers is to offer a lower price. For immigrants to find employers, they have to offer themselves at lower wages than American workers are presently earning. And if Americans are to keep their jobs, they have to match these lower wages.

It is true that when immigrants try to enter particular occupations, they may find willing employers only if they offer themselves at a lower wage than that which existing employees are receiving. *But this totally ignores the beneficial secondary effects which will then be operating in the market.* Costs of production will now be lower in these particular sectors of the economy (because of the lower wage costs). The lower costs will mean greater profits to be earned; and as employers expand their production, prices of consumer goods in these parts of the market will tend to decline over time as businesses compete for consumers to buy their greater output. The consuming public as a whole will be beneficiaries of the cheaper labor costs.

Furthermore, since some consumer goods will now cost less to buy, this will leave extra dollars in the pockets of consumers. They will now have the financial wherewithal to increase their demand for other products they previously could not afford to buy. This will raise the demand for workers in those sectors of the economy in which consumer demand will have gone up. To attract workers into these parts of the economy, employers will have to offer potential employees higher wages. Thus, for consumers in general, numerous goods and services will be less expensive; and for many workers, there will be an increased demand (and higher wages) for their labor services.

3. Large numbers of immigrants cannot easily be absorbed into American society and culture. It is argued that if large numbers of immigrants are permitted entry into the U.S., it will be difficult to absorb them because of the language and cultural differences that would arise. Better to limit immigration to an annual small number, it is said, so that they can more easily be assimilated.

But with every previous wave of immigrants, the concern was expressed that the new group would not be able to adapt to American life. In the middle of the 19th century, for example, the concern was that "those Germans" would not learn English and that they tended to live in ethnic enclaves with other Germans. Yet history has demonstrated that within one generation, both the immigrants and their children have rapidly become "Americanized." A recent case are the Vietnamese. In the span of just a few years, Vietnamese children have not only learned English, not only have become champions in the school spelling bees, but are also often found at the top of their classes.

The only things that can hamper the economic progress and cultural assimilation of immigrants are bad governmental policies: licensing restrictions that make it difficult to begin small businesses and enterprises; heavy tax burdens that destroy savings and investment incentives; welfare programs that draw people into the dead end of economic dependency upon the state; government schools, with their mandatory bilingual programs and socialist educational methods, that, more often than not, make it difficult for the children of immigrants to learn English rapidly and to adapt to their new country.

But the evils of governmental policies should not be a rationale or excuse for denying human beings the right to migrate and live where they wish. Rather, such evils provide the arguments for eliminating those governmental interventions.

The German free-market economist Wilhelm Röpke once suggested:

> Modern nationalism and collectivism have, by the restriction of migration, perhaps come nearest to the "servile state." . . . Man can hardly be reduced more to a mere wheel in the clockwork of the national collectivist state than being deprived of his freedom to move. . . . Feeling that he belongs now to his nation, body and soul, he will be more easily subdued to the obedient state serf which nationalist and collectivist governments demand.

We can only hope that Röpke's pessimism is ill-founded, that the spirit of freedom will never be extinguished, no matter how confining and encompassing the power of the state. But how much better it would be if the United States once again completely embodied the glorious vision of the right of free immigration expressed by the Statue of Liberty: "Give me your tired, your poor, your huddled masses, yearning to breathe free."

This essay appeared in the June 1991 issue of Freedom Daily, *published by The Future of Freedom Foundation.*

15

Locking Out the Immigrant

by Jacob G. Hornberger

America of the 1800s was a unique society in the history of man. People could engage in virtually any economic enterprise without permission of their public officials. People could become as wealthy as they wanted, and there was nothing the government could do about it. They could dispose of their money in any way they saw fit. And they could travel anywhere they desired without a passport or other evidence of governmental consent. This is what it once meant to be an American. This is what it once meant to be free.

But perhaps the most unusual aspect of American society of the 1800s was that reflected by the Statue of Liberty: free immigration. For this was a society in which the citizenry prohibited their public officials from interfering with the right of people everywhere to come to the United States to live and work.

What was the result of this unusual society—a society without income taxation, welfare, social security, licensing, passports, subsidies, economic regulations, and immigration restrictions? The result was the most economically prosperous nation in the history of man! And this despite the fact that thousands of penniless immigrants, many of whom could not speak English, were flooding American shores every day.

But prosperity for the poor was not the real significance of our ancestors' policy of freedom of immigration. The true significance is a much more profound one. For the first time in history, oppressed

91

and persecuted people everywhere had hope—hope that if they were able to escape the tyranny under which they suffered, there was a place which would accept them. America was a beacon—a beacon of liberty which shone through the darkness of oppression, persecution, and tyranny throughout the world—a beacon which lit the hearts of millions who knew that if they could just escape, there was a nation, albeit faraway, to which they could flee.

But no longer—and not for many decades. While the Statue of Liberty is a nice place for tourists to visit, it now stands as a sad reminder of the rejection and abandonment by 20th-century Americans of the principles of liberty on which our nation was founded. And while the welfare-state, planned-economy way of life most clearly evidences this rejection and abandonment, the consequences, while bad, have not been as evil and horrible as those resulting from the abandonment of the principles of free immigration.

We must never forget that citizens are responsible for wrongdoing by their own government—even when they consciously choose to ignore it. The best-known example in recent times of conscious disregard of wrongdoing by one's own government involved the German people in the 1930s—when Hitler embarked on his policy of extermination of the Jews. Most Americans believe that under same or similar circumstances, the people of this nation would act differently. Unfortunately, they are wrong. Because what Americans have never been taught in their public schools is that the American government, as well as other Western governments (including Britain, Canada, and most of Latin America), through their control of immigration sealed all avenues of Jewish escape from the Holocaust.

The sordid facts and details are set forth in two books: *While Six Million Died: A Chronicle of American Apathy* by Arthur D. Morse, first published in 1967, and *The Holocaust Conspiracy: An International Policy of Genocide* by William R. Perl, published in 1989. Morse was executive producer of "CBS Reports" and the winner of numerous broadcasting awards. Perl served as a lieutenant colonel in the U.S. Army Intelligence Service, worked in the Prosecution Branch of the War Crimes trials, and later taught at George Washington University.

An American cannot read these two books without total revulsion at the reaction of his own government to Hitler's policies against the Jews. Both authors detail the methods by which American politicians and bureaucrats, while maintaining an appearance of great humanitarianism, used immigration policies to prevent Germany's Jews from escaping to the United States. Morse writes:

In 1938 the Nazis burned every synagogue in the nation, shattered the windows of every Jewish establishment, hauled twenty-five thousand innocent people to concentration camps, and fined the Jews 1,000,000,000 marks for the damage.

Five days later, at a White House press conference a reporter asked the President, "Would you recommend a relaxation of our immigration restrictions so that the Jewish refugees could be received in this country?"

"This is not in contemplation," replied the President. "We have the quota system."

The United States not only insisted upon its immigration law throughout the Nazi era, but administered it with severity and callousness. In spite of unprecedented circumstances, the law was constricted so that even its narrow quotas were not met. The lamp remained lifted beside the golden door, but the flame had been extinguished and the door was padlocked.

And Perl writes:

Anti-Semitism . . . was certainly a part of the anti-immigration mood of the country, but it was not the sole cause. This was 1938, the U.S. was still on the fringes of the 1929 depression, and fear that newcomers would take away jobs needed from those already in the country was genuine. The fact that newcomers mean also increased consumption, that many of them, as they actually did, created new jobs rather than occupy existing ones was not considered. . . .

President Roosevelt was first of all a politician, and a shrewd and ruthless one at that. He was not going to imperil his fragile coalition for moral or humanitarian reasons. He was not ready to put it to a test over an issue that, he knew, was loaded with emotion among supporters as well as opponents and which was in summary not popular at all. He was at that time preparing to run for an unprecedented third term of the presidency, and any rocking of the boat was out of the question. . . . Yet, it was necessary to keep up the image of a great liberal and humanitarian.

One of the most dramatic and tragic examples of the U.S. government's immigration policy against the Jews was evidenced by what has become known as "the voyage of damned." Just before war broke out in Europe, a German cruise ship loaded with almost 1,000 Jewish refugees left Germany and headed to Cuba—where friends and relatives of the passengers waited for their loved ones. When the ship arrived, the Cuban government refused to permit the Jews to disembark. When the ship began moving close to American waters, the United States Coast Guard closely followed to make certain that no Jew jumped ship and infiltrated America.

Since no other nations were willing to accept the refugees, the ship headed back to Germany where certain death awaited its passengers. At the last minute, England and some of the European nations reluctantly agreed to accept the refugees. Unfortunately, many of those who went to Europe were later killed under the Nazi occupation.

It is easy for present-day Americans to say, "We would never let that happen again." Yet, we continue to permit public officials to control immigration. And the results of control point only in the direction of future catastrophe.

The U.S. government rightly criticizes the Soviet Union for not letting Jews emigrate . . . but then is horrified at the prospect of having to let Soviet Jews enter the United States. And it rightly criticizes Vietnam for its oppressive society . . . but then is horrified at the prospect of having to let too many Vietnamese "boat people" enter the United States.

And on the southern border of the United States, good and honorable people of the Republic of Mexico have been incarcerated, year after year, in American concentration centers for committing the heinous "crime" of trying to sustain and improve their lives through labor. I personally have been inside these concentration centers and visited with these victims of 20th-century political tyranny, and I shall never forget the looks on their faces—looks which asked, "Why are you doing this to us?"

Free immigration is nothing to fear. As free-market economists have shown for years (i.e., Julian L. Simon's 1989 book, *The Economic Consequences of Immigration),* immigration is actually an economic boon to a society. Of course, fears of huge burdens associated with welfare, public schooling, and other aspects of the welfare state are a legitimate concern. But we should not use the welfare state as an excuse for rejecting free immigration; instead, we should use free- dom as a reason for ending both the welfare state and immigration controls—and for ending the real and potential evils associated with them.

As walls separating people are crumbling all over the world, it is time for us to tear down our walls. It is time for us to recapture the spirit of liberty which guided our American ancestors and to lead the world to the highest reaches of freedom ever known by man. It is time for us to let the world know that its beacon of liberty is once again lighted for its poor, its tired, its huddled masses yearning to breathe free!

This essay appeared in the June 1991 issue of Freedom Daily, *published by The Future of Freedom Foundation.*

16

In Defense of Free Migration

by Richard M. Ebeling

Right at this moment, hundreds, perhaps thousands, of Vietnamese are in the South China Sea. Some of them are heading for Hong Kong, others are heading for the Philippines or Malaysia or Singapore. But regardless of their destination, every one of those Vietnamese has made a choice. They have chosen to leave the land of their birth, their culture, their heritage and make a new start. They have decided that their homeland has become intolerable for themselves and their children. They hope and pray for a better life than the one they leave behind under the choking hand of socialist statism.

It is estimated that hundreds of these Vietnamese will never see land again. Faulty navigation, lack of food and fresh water, or disease will bring them to their deaths. Many probably could be saved. Ships will pass them by that could have taken them aboard and landed them in safety, but will not. The ship captains and owners are reluctant to give shelter and assistance, because they know that at whatever port at which they land they will be quarantined, inspected, and detained, for none of the Asian countries are willing to give free entrance to these new citizens of the world.

But even those Vietnamese who languish in detention camps in Malaysia or the Philippines are still better off than those countless people in Cambodia who had no chance of escape and were consumed in that human bonfire that served the ends of collectivist purity and so-called people's justice.

The Vietnamese refugees are not unique in their experience, either in facing oppression at home or in their decision to emigrate. Countless millions of others in the last two hundred years faced similar despotisms and chose to make a new life in a freer land.

What is different is that for most of those two hundred years there was at least one country that was open to those escaping from economic destitution, political oppression, or social rigidity. Today there no longer exists any nation whose gates are spread wide welcoming newcomers. Today the gates are closed, and only political pressure or public shock and indignation can push them ajar for a fortunate handful.

The inscription on the Statue of Liberty may still read: "Give me your tired, your poor, your huddled masses yearning to breathe free. . . . I lift my lamp beside the golden door," but it stands there as a cruel joke to those who see the "golden door" barred to their entrance.

Almost no other country on the face of the earth has had its history so closely tied with and dependent upon the free movement of men and women as the United States.

In the Declaration of Independence, one of the stated grievances against the British Crown was governmental barriers to freedom of movement. The King "has endeavored to prevent the population of these States," charged the signers of the Declaration. They accused the British government of "obstructing the Laws of Naturalization of Foreigners; refusing to pass [laws] to encourage their migration hither, and raising the conditions of new Appropriations of Lands."

Not long after the Declaration was signed, the principle was generalized when Thomas Jefferson wrote of "the natural right which all men have of relinquishing the country in which birth or other accident may have thrown them, and seeking subsistence and happiness wheresoever they may be able, or hope to find them."

Since the first English settlers reached America in 1607, almost 50 million people have migrated to the United States.

A good many of those 50 million came to America to escape from persecution, oppression, and the control of the State. In the 19th century, four million Irish came across the Atlantic, leaving behind potato famines and British imperialism. Between 1850 and 1900, five million Germans found a new home in America, many of them escaping from the convulsions and high conscription rates caused by Bismarck's wars of the 1860s and early 1870s. Well over one million Poles arrived before World War I, leaving behind acute poverty in territory controlled by Russia and the suppression of Polish culture and nationality in the portions of Poland under German domination. The same story can be repeated in the case of almost every other national group that contributed an ingredient to the American melting pot.

For every immigrant, America offered a new beginning, a second chance without the oppressive air of privilege and power. A Swedish immigrant wrote home in the 1880s that his "cap [is not] worn out from lifting it in the presence of gentlemen. There is no class distinction between high and low, rich and poor, no make-believe, no 'title-sickness' or artificial ceremonies. . . . Everybody lives in peace and prosperity."

In the 19th century, it was mostly young men who would first arrive from another country, attempt to make a living and send money back home. For example, of the Italians who came to the United States, 78 percent were male; and in the case of the Greeks, 95 percent of the immigrants were male. In the 1850s Irish immigrants were sending over one million dollars a year to friends and relatives in Ireland, with half of that amount being sent in the form of prepaid tickets to assist others in coming to America. In the late 19th century and early 20th century, the estimate is that 25 to 75 percent of all immigrants coming to America did so with money sent from compatriots already in the United States. Almost every one of these immigrant groups tended to start at the bottom of the economic ladder, taking the jobs considered undignified or undesirable by others. And almost every immigrant usually began his start in America by settling in that section of the city predominantly occupied by members of the same nationality, culture, and language.

Those who wish to immigrate to the United States today are fundamentally no different from those who came to America a hundred years ago. The Mexican who slips into the United States and resides here as an "illegal alien" tends to be a young adult male looking for work; when he finds a job, he sends a good portion of his earnings back to his family in Mexico. He usually has had no more than five years of schooling and probably speaks little or no English. The aliens tend to gravitate to the lowest-paying occupations that others prefer to turn down, and it is estimated that twenty percent of them make below the minimum wage. They live in various Mexican-American communities around the country, and except for work come into very little contact with "Anglo" Americans.

But there is a unique difference between the 19th-century immigrant and the 20th-century "illegal" immigrant. The earlier immigrants worked in a relatively free and open society and could expect in a generation or two to advance themselves economically and socially compared to the living standards in the "old country" and compared to when they first began to live and work in America.

The 20th-century illegal immigrants have no similar future to look forward to. They have only the present, and it is a present that yields nothing but fear and uncertainty—uncertainty that at any moment they may be discovered by the immigration authorities and deported, and the fear that any resistance or refusal to accept the terms set for them by their employers may result in their being turned in to the authorities.

However, the really fundamental difference between the 19th-century and 20th-century immigrants concerns the ideological undercurrents present, then and now. In the 19th century, freedom of movement was generally seen as an integral part of a philosophy and policy of free trade. Just as the free movement of goods across frontiers was seen as the method by which individuals of the respective countries of the world could benefit from their comparative productive advantages, free movement of people was seen as the method by which individuals—each pursuing his own personal interest—could assure that labor would come to be distributed among the various geographical areas in the pattern that was most conducive to private and social prosperity.

The same economic influences that enticed owners of capital to shift their factors of production from one use to another tended to operate on those who supplied labor services, as well. Those countries that suffered from low productivity and low wages would "export" workers to other parts of the globe where wages were relatively higher and productive prospects were likely to raise the income positions of those who moved into the higher-wage areas.

The advantages from the transfer of workers would tend to benefit everyone. In the case of the workers who immigrated, it offered the opportunity to compete in an alternative labor market where their relative income share could be larger. Free immigration benefited those who remained in the home country; the shrinkage of the domestic labor force due to the emigration of others made labor a relatively more scarce resource in the market and tended to raise the level of wages in the home country.

The country into which the immigrants flowed benefited from the move, as well. The increase in the workforce diminished the scarcity of labor services in various lines of production. The lowering of costs and the availability of more hands for production activities meant an intensification of the division of labor, a general increase in productivity and the opportunity for the production of totally new goods and services that had been beyond the reach of consumers in the past because of the lack of manpower to provide them.

The economic and social principles of laissez-faire and laissez-passer were intertwined and inseparable. The advantage that necessarily followed from the unhampered exchange of goods across the borders of different countries could not attain its maximum potential unless the free movement of goods was matched by the free movement of labor and capital to where the greatest economic advantage was anticipated.

The advantages of laissez-faire and laissez-passer, however, require not only freedom of movement, but flexibility of wages and prices that enables an adjustment to change and progress. Need for adjustment can arise either from the demand side or the supply side.

If the pattern of relative consumer demand were to change, some industries would find their profitability diminished. A successful adaptation to the new circumstances would require a shifting of resources—including labor—from those areas where profitability had declined to those areas where it had increased. Resistance to lower wages, or reluctance to change occupations when the relative demand for a product declines, can only result in unemployment, a decline in output and income, and a general fall in the economic well-being of the country as a whole. The unwillingness of a few to adapt to new market circumstances rebounds to the disadvantage of all.

An increase in the availability of scarce resources necessitates shifts in the relative distribution of labor among industries, as well. Labor is not a homogeneous glob; there are different types and degrees of labor skills, just as there are different types of capital goods and consumer goods. The arrival of new workers through the process of immigration means that in particular lines of employment, the increased labor supply will put downward pressure on some wages. To remain employed in their present occupation, established workers would have to accept a lower rate of remuneration. If they find this unacceptable, then they may have to shift into other lines of work. While this job shift takes place, wages in the industries into which they shift may be lowered, as well. This, in turn, may mean that existing workers in these other industries have to accept lower wages.

But regardless of the particular types of changes and ramifications an increase in the labor force brings about, the general long-run outcome will reflect itself in greater output and, through an intensification of the division of labor, a widening of choices and opportunities for all individuals, both as consumers and producers.

The expansion of rigidities through government-bestowed privilege and monopoly conflicts by its very nature with the free flow of men and material. To the extent that the protection of particular groups becomes the goal of the state, restriction on the potential competition of newcomers must be imposed and enforced.

In the libertarian society, national borders—to the extent that governments may still exist—would merely be administrative boundaries designating areas of responsibility for the protection of life and property. In the interventionist state, boundaries become lines of demarcation designating respective areas of privilege and power. As Wilhelm Röpke vividly expressed it, in the present era of nationalism and interventionism, "national frontiers have been changed into barbed wire fences."

When the welfare and employment of specially privileged groups becomes the duty of the state, protectionist quotas and tariff walls are soon joined by barriers to immigration. The arguments often used to support immigration controls easily bear this out. It is often said that if there were unrestricted immigration, welfare rolls would climb, neighborhoods would no longer maintain their present identities and qualities, and jobs would be stolen from American labor.

The fear of a swarm of immigrant welfare addicts is the logical terror of those who either operate or live off the dole. A crushing load of additional welfare recipients could easily arouse the wrath of the taxpayers and bring about the end of the welfare system. This is the logical fear of those who envisage the collapse of an economic privilege if too many other people should clamor for the same benefits. In fact, historically, the immigrant has usually been a young, hard-working individual who has requested nothing more than a chance to make his own way. For example, in a recent investigation of 9,132 welfare cases in San Diego County, only ten illegal immigrants were found on the rolls.

Neither neighborhoods nor their qualities can be eternally preserved. Values, preferences and personalities all change over time. Some land and property values grow and others decline, but regardless of which it is, this is the natural result of the free choices of acting individuals. It is as illusory to think that cities and neighborhoods can be frozen and maintained in their present form as it would have been to try to prevent natural forces turning bustling Western boomtowns into decaying ghost towns. Those who attempt to use immigration barriers and other methods to resist change are not only fighting against the future, but the present, as well.

The fears of labor unions that a flood of immigrants will cause economic misery and mass unemployment is totally illusory, as well. In a country such as the United States, more hands will almost always tend to mean more production and prosperity. Unemployment follows in the wake of an increased labor force only if rigidity and privilege prevent the changes in relative prices, wages, and employment that must occur if the benefits of immigration are to be reaped.

The most detrimental consequence of immigration barriers, it should always be remembered, is the personal tragedy, the economic misery, and political despair of those who find themselves locked into oppressive societies with no chance of escape. Wilhelm Röpke has suggested:

> Modern nationalism and collectivism have, by the restriction of migration, perhaps come nearest to the "servile state." . . . Man can hardly be reduced more to a mere wheel in the clockwork of the national collectivist state than by being deprived of his freedom to move. . . . Feeling that he belongs now to his nation, body and soul, he will be more easily subdued to the obedient state serf which nationalist and collectivist governments demand.

We can only hope that Röpke's deep pessimism is ill-founded, that the spirit of freedom will never be extinguished, no matter how confining and all-encompassing the power of the nation-state. But how much more glorious if the motto on the Statue of Liberty once again embodied truth, rather than hypocrisy, and America once again said to every nation: "Give me your tired, your poor, your huddled masses yearning to breathe free."

This article first appeared in Volume XII, No. 2 (March/April 1979), of The Libertarian Forum. *It was later reprinted by The Libertarian Alliance in London, England.*

17

The Case Against
the Immigration Laws

by Richard M. Ebeling

Economic privilege is never so visible as it is during periods of crisis and depression. What are merely lone voices crying for protection from the rigors of the marketplace during normal times become a chorus of special interests begging for high tariffs and import quotas to camouflage their inefficiencies. Rarely has the state turned a deaf ear to their pleas. More often than not, reason and consumer interest have failed in their attempt to withstand the pressure of those who have striven for gain through government intervention.

"The Protectionist creed rises like a weed in every soil," lamented the Classical economist Walter Bagehot over a hundred years ago. "Every nation wishes prosperity for some conspicuous industry. At what cost to the consumer, by what hardship to less conspicuous industries, that prosperity is obtained, it does not care ... the visible picture of the smoking chimney absorbs the whole mind."

The economic recession of the past few years has revived the ideology of protectionism once again. The steel industry won limitations on the importation of European and Japanese steel by ranting about "dumping." American farmers mass at the Mexican border chanting incantations to ward off the flow of cheap food from south of the Rio Grande. And the trade unions conjure up the image of millions of unemployed workers if protectionist policies are not enacted to "save" American jobs.

All of these myths have been answered and demolished hundreds of times over. In every case, logic has refuted the conclusions of the protectionist rationale. And in every instance, it has been demonstrated that the purpose of the restrictions were to preserve the economic status of some, while victimizing others.

The most insidious form of protectionism, however, does not pertain to the barriers placed in the way of the free movement of goods. As harmful and as illogical as these interventions are, none cause the human hardship and misery that immigration restrictions impose.

The importance of the principle of laissez-passer was understood early in American history. It was clearly enunciated by Thomas Jefferson, when he insisted upon "the natural right which all men have of relinquishing the country in which birth or other accident may have thrown them, and seeking subsistence and happiness wheresoever they may be able, or may hope to find them."

Leaving behind poverty, despotism, war, and conscription, millions came to the American shores, to build "a nation of immigrants." Between 1800 and 1840, about 800,000 immigrants arrived in the United States, of whom 750,000 remained in America. And from the middle of the 19th century until the 1930s, gross immigration tended to exceed 200,000 per year (with the number exceeding 1,000,000 per year on six occasions).

Of course, this inflow of immigrants was not without opposition. There were those who feared the "alien" element and the "impurities" that were "polluting" the American soil. In 1903, John R. Commons, a leader of the American Institutionalists, begged for limitations on the immigration of particular ethnic groups. "Our democratic theories and forms of government were fashioned by but one of the many races and peoples," Commons insisted. "That race, the so-called Anglo-Saxon, developed them out of its own insular experience unhampered by inroads of alien stock."

But arguments such as Commons had already been shown the contempt they deserved during the heyday of the Know-Nothing Party in the mid-19th century. In 1855, Abraham Lincoln expressed his disgust with this "Americanist" philosophy. "When the Know-Nothings get control," Lincoln said, "it [the Declaration of Independence] will read 'all men are created equal except negroes and foreigners and catholics.' When it comes to this, I should prefer emigrating to some country where they make no pretense of loving liberty—to Russia, for instance, where despotism can be taken pure, and without the basic alloy of hypocrisy. . . ."

Now, in fact, it is difficult to see what exactly that American "stock" was that Commons and others were so concerned about preserving and protecting. To the contrary, America's history has been one of ever-new faces and peoples. America has truly been a nation of immigrants.

In the 1830s, 500,000 new arrivals touched upon American soil. In the 1840s, that number increased to 1.5 million, with an additional 2.6 million added in the 1850s. By the turn of the century, ten million people of foreign birth were living in the United States. And out of a total U.S. population of slightly over 76 million, 26 million were the children of foreign-born parents.

During the period 1900-1920, approximately 13.5 million more immigrants arrived in America. It was only the post-World War I hysteria about foreign subversives and the influence of vested interests that brought that movement to an end. As the historian Charles Beard aptly put it, "The gates of the once wide-open 'asylum for the oppressed of all lands' had been brought together with a bang. . . ."

In the period 1931 to 1945, only 900,000 new people were allowed entrance. In the post-World War II era, the fear of foreigners dampened slightly and 4.4 million were allowed to enter the country between 1945 and 1965.

This multitude of humanity, however, had not been the product of one culture, but of many. In vast numbers they came from Britain, Ireland, Germany, Italy, the Balkans, Russia, Mexico, and Asia. America was not the child of one racial or cultural strain, but rather the offspring of diversity and change. Not bound by one cultural heritage or one concept of social strata, America developed precisely because of its multicultural fluidity—constantly fed by newcomers supplying fresh spirit and potential.

America became a wide-open—yes, let's not be afraid to use that cliché—"land of opportunity." It was clearly seen by the Italian classical liberal Gugliemo Ferrero. At the turn of the century, he wrote:

> [T]hanks to the almost complete lack of intellectual protectionism—that is, of academical degrees which ensure the monopoly of certain professions—thanks, in consequence to the lack of a government *curriculum* of unprofitable studies, America is exempt from an intellectual proletariat and from the *declasses*, the chronic disease of the middle classes in Europe. Let him who can do a thing well step forward and do it, no one will question where he learnt it: such is the degree required of an American engineer, barrister, clerk, or employee.

At the heart of the anti-immigration sentiment, however, has been the belief that the newcomers glut the labor market, lower the level of wages, and rain economic misery upon the domestic population. The racist elements merely serve as the convenient method of separating "them" from "us." This is most obviously seen in the case of the Chinese. Within two years of the California gold discoveries in the late 1840s, at least 25,000 Chinese had come across the Pacific to serve as the manpower in the goldfields and mines. The number of Chinese brought over soon increased with the building of the Western railroads. Comprising nine percent of California's population between 1860 and 1880, the Chinese were accused of lowering the wages of white workers. The Caucasian clamors reached levels of hysteria after 1869 with the completion of the Union Pacific Railroad. With European-born workers often taking the lead, the anti-Chinese feeling resulted in riots, plundering, and murder.

In 1882 (four years before the Statue of Liberty was given to the United States), the first immigration laws were imposed upon the Chinese. From 40,000 Chinese immigrants in 1882, the number tumbled to ten in 1887. Even to stay in the United States every Chinese required the sworn testimony of a white man. Writing in a recent issue of *Society*, Betty Lee Sung explained that "before 1943 Chinese immigrants were not permitted to become citizens no matter how long they had resided in this country. . . . They were forbidden by the Alien Land Acts to own land. . . . They were also denied the right to intermarry in many western states."

More recently, the unfair labor competition arguments have been directed against the potential Mexican immigrant (though more generally to all immigrants). With a force of 9,600 men and a budget of $250 million, the Immigration and Naturalization Service (INS) every year sends its men scurrying along the U.S.-Mexican border rounding up "illegals" and sending them back to a Mexican economy that suffers from high inflation and an unemployment rate of 20 to 30 percent. In 1973, the INS deported 655,928 of these "aliens;" in 1974, 788,145; in 1975, 766,600; and in 1977, the number exceeded one million.

However, for every one potential immigrant captured at the border, the INS admits three to five others escape detection and join the estimated seven to 12 million illegal aliens already residing in the United States.

Thus, the logical step is to ask what exactly are the economic consequences that follow from the free flow of people from one geographical area to another. Let us first abstract from the rest of the world and inquire into how a labor force is distributed within our own country.

Within America, freedom of trade and freedom of movement are established principles. At any given moment in time, consumers are spending their income in a manner that reflects their relative preferences for various goods and services sold on the market. In turn, producers are purchasing various factors of production— including labor—in the anticipation that the costs incurred in hiring them will be compensated when their products are sold on the market. Workers, in turn, look for the best job opportunities that they can find, based upon their view of which employers are offering the highest wages and best working conditions, given the particular skills that they possess.

Producers establish their businesses in various parts of America based upon, among other things, the location of raw materials necessary for their production activities and the transportation costs that must be paid to get the products to their markets. The laborers will, to the extent that they are willing and able to bear the cost of moving from one location to another, move from one job to another in such a way that the same wage rate tends to be paid in all parts of the country for each of the respective types of labor. (Unions, the cost of living, welfare benefits, unemployment insurance, and other such differences, of course, might lead people to act differently.)

Suppose there occurs an increase in the demand for the products produced in a particular part of America—in California, for instance—and a decrease in the demand for products made in, say, New York. The anticipation of a higher selling price for their products will induce these California producers to offer higher wages, to attract more workers into their industries. On the other hand, the fall in the demand for New York products will result in those producers offering wages lower than before. The fall in New York wage rates will create an incentive for some of those workers to migrate to California where higher wages are now available. As more and more workers move to California, the increase in the labor supply will begin to lower California wages. And as more and more workers leave New York, the decrease in the labor supply will raise New York wages. The process will come to an end when the wages received in New York and California are roughly equivalent and the incentive for migration has disappeared.

Of course, there will be some individuals who, because of nonmonetary attachments to their hometown or home state, may choose not to move when a change in wage rates occurs between two locations. Thus, the people residing near Lake Tahoe may decide to remain there, even though higher wages could be received somewhere else. In turn, some people may choose to move from somewhere else without monetary incentives; a desired change in climate or a disapproval of the ideas or morals of the people around them may stimulate immigration to another part of America.

Immigration to California due to these nonmonetary reasons will tend to cause lower wages there. But it will, on the other hand, set off market forces to correct the imbalance. Other areas of America will be offering wages that now are higher than in California. For some residents of California, this will act as an incentive to move elsewhere, until wages are once again adjusted throughout America.

The same principles apply when the geographical area being considered incorporates more than one country. This is most clearly seen when we consider the case of Mexico and the United States. Prior to the U.S. Immigration Act of 1924, movement between the two countries was completely open. A major emigration from Mexico occurred during the decade 1910-1919. The initial cause was the extreme violence in Mexico during that country's revolutionary war. However, labor shortages (particularly in agriculture) began to develop once the United States entered the First World War. In 1910, 17,760 Mexicans moved into the United States. In 1919, the number increased to 28,844 new arrivals. It peaked in 1923, with the movement of 62,709 Mexicans to areas north of the Rio Grande. But the 1924 immigration act soon brought this torrent to a halt, and by 1933, only 1,000 Mexicans were being allowed into the United States each year. Under the 1968 immigration act, only 120,000 people from the Western Hemisphere were allowed into the United States annually, with Mexico being allowed a maximum of 40,000 out of that total. (Of course, the restrictions on free movement have not been totally the fault of the United States. Under Article 123 of the 1917 Mexican constitution, the unregulated hiring of Mexican citizens by foreign nations had been prohibited.)

The barriers placed in the way of free immigration have prevented the adjustment of wage rates between the United States and Mexico. Under laissez-passer, the discrepancy between what was paid for one type of labor in the United States and what was received for the same type of labor in Mexico would act as an incentive for workers to move, until economic adjustments were made. Instead, this rigidity imposed on the market by the governments concerned has caused the wage differentials to widen more and more.

In 1976, the average hourly wage for agricultural labor in the United States was $2.66; in Mexico, the average hourly wage in the agricultural industry was equivalent to $0.45. In 1977, U.S. manufacturing industries paid, on the average, $5.65 an hour; in Mexico, the equivalent wage was $1.58 per hour. The hourly average wage for American construction workers in 1974 was $6.54; in Mexico, it was $0.84 an hour. In 1973, in the United States, the average hourly salary on the principal railroads was $5.40 (on local railroads and bus lines it averaged $3.97 an hour); in Mexico, the equivalent wage rate in the transportation industry was $0.94 an hour.

While Mexican immigrants in the United States may earn less than the national average in these areas, they will still earn much more than they would have in Mexico.

It is not surprising, then, that many Mexican workers desire to immigrate to the United States. And what would be the terrible consequences if the gates were opened to these Mexicans? In those industries in the American economy that would be affected by the larger labor supply, a lowering of wage rates would occur. Some of the workers in those industries might have to shift to work in other established firms. However, there exist alternative possibilities, as well. Since labor, like any other commodity, is a scarce resource, the larger labor force in America could enable a greater intensification of the division of labor—thus raising the productivity of workers in general. The larger supply of workers would also enable the application of labor towards the production of goods and services that previously could not be supplied at all because of the scarcity of hands. As Stephen Chapman points out in his excellent article, "Let the Aliens In," in *The Washington Monthly* (July-August 1977):

> Many of the jobs held by illegal aliens are the kind that few Americans would accept, regardless of their skills. A California businessman who hires illegals told *New West* magazine, "If you pulled out every illegal alien in Los Angeles at midnight tonight, you would wake up tomorrow morning in a town without busboys, maids, or parking-lot attendants."

Chapman cites a case in San Diego in which the State Human Resources Agency could not fill 2,154 jobs "made available by the deportation of illegal workers."

The flexibility of wage rates—a necessary ingredient for a stable and progressive economy—has been something vehemently resisted by the trade unions. Their opposition to free immigration has always been a key element in their drive for union privileges. "The oft-referred to 'miracle' of the high wages in the United States and Australia," Ludwig von Mises has observed, "may be explained simply by the policy of trying to prevent a new immigration . . . that the unions in all those countries which have more favorable conditions of production, relatively fewer workers and thus higher wages, seek to prevent an influx of workers from less favored lands. . . ."

At the turn of the century, for example, Samuel Gompers insisted that "as these immigrants flooded basic industries they threatened to destroy our standards." Gompers proudly added: "[A]s a nation we began to consider policies of regulation. The labor movement was among the first organizations to urge such policies. . . ."

The restrictions pertain, however, not only to unskilled labor and farm workers, but to all types of skilled labor, as well. In fact, there are thirty-two "exclusion" categories expressly forbidding individuals with particular talents from residing and working in the United States. Pressure from the American medical profession has resulted in foreign medical graduates being placed on that restriction list. Laurier B. McDonald, a Texas lawyer long involved with illegal alien cases, has pointed out that existing law "places physicians in the same category as prostitutes, thieves, idiots and subversives."

The immigration laws have both seen and unseen consequences. The obvious effects are evident all around the world. They are seen in the state of starvation that is the human condition in dozens of countries; they are seen in the cardboard hovels that many Mexicans call "home," in the area surrounding Tijuana and Ensenada; they are seen on the faces of the desperate individuals who time and time again make the vain attempt to enter the United States—both legally and illegally; and they are seen in the mass attempts to escape from various despotisms and in the bickerings among nations over who will have to take these refugees—most recently in the cases of the Ugandan Asians, and with the Vietnamese and Cambodians.

The unseen burden of immigration laws falls upon those who illegally reside in the United States. As Stephen Chapman wrote in his *Washington Monthly* article:

> The illegal alien's outlaw status undercuts his bargaining power and compels him to accept nearly anything his employer chooses to inflict on him, from low pay to long hours to poor working conditions. . . . If he is maltreated, defrauded, or injured on the job, he is not likely to seek legal redress. All the pressures on the illegal worker encourage him to do what he's told, take whatever pay he's given and keep his mouth shut. . . . If he complains, his employer can fire him or even have him arrested by the INS.

While it is the trade union and professional association members who benefit from the barriers that prevent the arrival of new competition, the immigration laws rebound to the advantage of those business firms that hire the illegal aliens once they have entered the country. In the grasp of these employers is a pool of labor ripe for economic exploitation. The life of the illegal aliens become a nightmare of fear—fear of the demands of the employers on one side and the fear of apprehension by the state on the other. The incentive for exploiting these workers is reinforced by the laws that make it a felony to be an illegal alien, but not to hire one.

Economic reality and basic human justice, therefore, call for the immediate removal of all immigration and emigration restrictions.

One might object that there still remains the problem of the welfare state. Just as the differential in welfare payments between various states has enticed a migration of people to the high-paying welfare areas in America, the same process might occur among nations. But surely this is more an argument against the continuance of the welfare state itself than against the free flow of people. The existence of one set of statist impositions should not be the rationale for imposing yet another set.

Moreover, as Chapman has pointed out, the picture of the illegal alien as a welfare-grasping bum is viciously unjust: "Aliens, like most immigrants, generally appear eager to accept work of any kind because of the social stigma they attach to not working, the improvement it represents over jobs in their native countries, and the hope of advancement." Moreover, a Department of Labor study by David North and Marion Houston reported the following in 1976:

> This group of illegal alien workers were significantly more likely to have participated in tax-paying systems (many of which are automatic) than to have used tax-supported programs ... while 77 percent of the study group reported that they had had social security taxes and 73 percent reported that they had federal income taxes withheld. Only 27 percent used hospitals or clinics, four per cent collected one or more weeks of unemployment insurance, four percent had children in U.S. schools, one percent secured food stamps, and .5 percent secured welfare payments.

In San Diego County, the best estimates are that the county's cost in "social services" to illegal aliens is about $2 million, while the aliens' taxes amount to more than $48 million. To this, Chapman appropriately responds: "Instead of aliens being a burden to the rest of us, it's the rest of us who are a burden to the aliens."

Even those who should know better fall into the collectivist snares. In a letter to the *London Times* on February 11, 1978, Professor Friedrich A. Hayek—himself an immigrant several times in his life—praised the British Conservative leader Margaret Thatcher for her call for stringent immigration controls. "While I look forward, as an ultimate ideal, to a state of affairs in which national boundaries have ceased to be obstacles to the free movement of men," Hayek declared, "I believe that within any period with which we can now be concerned, any attempt to realize it would lead to a revival of strong nationalist sentiments."

The problem facing the world is not the possibility of a revival of nationalism and other collectivist atavisms, but rather that they already dominate all social thought and policy. We cannot passively wait for the day when mankind will somehow "naturally" evolve out of collectivism. It must be resisted and abolished—and that includes the abolition of immigration barriers and the human suffering that they cause.

We must embrace the philosophy expressed by the French classical liberal, Emile Levasseur:

> As a free and unfettered commercial intercourse between two countries is advantageous to both, for by the exchange of their commodities the producer and the consumer are both benefited, so also must the unrestricted circulation of the human race be advantageous to all countries concerned . . . it . . . must be viewed in the more comprehensive and enlightened scope of the enormous benefits it confers upon the human race at large.

If human liberty is to be complete, laissez-faire, the freedom to trade, must be at long last matched by laissez-passer, the freedom to move. The standard of the free society must once again be raised high, and America must once more become, as it was in the beginning, the "nation of immigrants," and the land of individual liberty.

This essay appeared in the June 1978 issue of The Libertarian Review.

18

Value Added

by Ron K. Unz

T he evidence shows that the immigration of the last thirty years has been a large net benefit for America, as well as an important source of strength for political parties espousing conservative principles.

Anyone walking the streets of our major cities sees that the majority of the shops are owned and operated by immigrant entrepreneurs—Korean grocery stores, Indian newsstands, Chinese restaurants. Most of these shops simply would not exist without immigrant families willing to put in long hours of poorly paid labor to maintain and expand them, in the process improving our cities. In Los Angeles, the vast majority of hotel and restaurant workers are hardworking Hispanic immigrants, most of them here illegally, and anyone who believes that these unpleasant jobs would otherwise be filled by natives (either black or white) is living in a fantasy world.

The same principle applies to nearly all the traditional lower-rung working-class jobs in Southern California, including the nannies and gardeners whose widespread employment occasionally embarrasses the Zoë Bairds of this world (even as it facilitates their careers). The only means of making a job as restaurant busboy even remotely attractive to a native American would be to raise the wage to $10 or $12 per hour, at which point the job would cease to exist.

Since most newcomers tend to be on the lower end of the wage scale, and since many have children in the public schools, they do tend to cost local government more in services than they pay in sales and income taxes. (The same could probably be said for most

115

members of the working class with young children.) This is the basis of California Governor Pete Wilson's lawsuit over the "costs" to California of illegal immigration. Yet the real culprit is our outrageously inefficient public-school system. Furthermore, because of their age profile, even working-class immigrants generally pay much more in federal taxes (primarily Social Security withholding) than they receive in federal benefits. So we might equally say that immigrants are helping us balance the federal budget.

Immigrants are crucial not just to industries that rely on cheap, low-skilled labor. Silicon Valley, which is home to my own software company, depends on immigrant professionals to maintain its technological edge. A third of all the engineers and chip designers here are foreign born, and if they left, America's computer industry would probably go with them. In fact, many of the most important technology companies of the 1980s, in California and elsewhere, were created by immigrants, including Sun Microsystems, AST, ALR, Applied Materials, Everex, and Gupta. Borland International, a software company worth hundreds of millions of dollars, was founded by Philippe Kahn, an illegal immigrant. These immigrant companies have generated hundreds of thousands of good jobs in California for native Americans and have provided billions of dollars in tax revenues. Without a continuing influx of immigrants, America's tremendous and growing dominance in sunrise industries would rapidly be lost. . . .

While several of the most parasitic sectors of American society—politicians, government bureaucrats, lawyers—are almost entirely filled with native Americans, each year one-third to one-half of the student winners of the Westinghouse Science Talent Search (America's most prestigious high-school science competition) come from immigrant families, often quite impoverished. Many of America's elite universities have student bodies that are 20 per cent Asian, with immigrants often accounting for half or more of the science and engineering students.

***Ron K. Unz**, a Silicon Valley entrepreneur, received more than a third of the vote in his 1994 Republican primary challenge to California Governor Pete Wilson. This is an excerpt from an article by the same title that appeared in the November 7, 1994, issue of* National Review. *© 1994 by National Review, Inc., 150 East 35th Street, New York, NY 10016. Reprinted by permission.*

19

Immigration and Somalia

by Gregory F. Rehmke

Calls are rising to send American troops into the cities, towns and villages of Serbia, Croatia, and Bosnia. Perhaps not far in the future, Russia and Ukraine will collapse, leading to calls for American troops to rush in and save the day. But is it possible that there is a better way to save the world?

There is a better idea, and it is simple and inexpensive: emigration and immigration. Or, to give it a more Biblical ring: "Let those people go! And let those people come!"

In the nineteenth century, oppressed and starving people were let go—and they came to America. Immigration powered the American economy, making it the fastest growing in the world. And emigration from heavily taxed and regulated old-world countries allowed their stagnant economies to better serve the remaining population.

Open-immigration policies that for over a century benefited the world and benefited America are today ignored or dismissed as unworkable. The only policy debates the public hears are those over whether immigration policy should be slightly more restrictive or slightly less restrictive. Or the public hears breathless debates over whether impoverished immigrants fled their repressive countries for "economic" or "political" reasons.

People see immigration as causing disarray and discomfort— they expect overloaded welfare agencies and jammed public schools. But such costs can be avoided or paid for by the immigrants themselves. The problem of poor immigrants jumping into welfare lines is better solved by eliminating welfare rather than stopping immigrants. Alternatively, a condition of immigration could be the following: "As a resident alien (as compared to an American citizen), you shall not be entitled to receive welfare." The same could be said with respect to public schools (which would be a benefit to the immigrant as well as society, since the immigrant's children would then have a better chance to receive a better education).

What about immigrants who might need an initial financial boost? As study after study has shown, philanthropy works best when it is voluntary—either from individuals or from organizations. Governmental assembly-line welfare programs tend to demean and dehumanize recipients. The small percentage of new immigrants who turn to welfare could easily be directed to privately funded support organizations within their community or to cultural and church organizations run by people from the immigrants' homelands.

In any case, few new immigrants are likely to demand welfare support. Poor people newly arrived in wealthy countries tend to work hard. What they lack in job skills, they make up in diligence. America looks different to them than it does to the average American, rich or poor. Imagine moving to another country where you were offered $100 an hour to sweep floors. And once you mastered their weird foreign language and learned some new skills, you believed you could make $500 to $1,000 an hour. Chances are you would work very hard. Well, that is what America looks like to immigrants from Latin America, formerly communist Europe, Asia and Africa. And that is why many, many people in these countries, especially young people, are eager to come to America. Wages here, even for the worst jobs, often pay ten to twenty times what jobs pay in poor countries (though expenses, of course, are much higher here as well).

For all the high-sounding talk Americans offer about saving the world, what our government ends up doing is sending diplomats, tax dollars and troops overseas. Much of the world, however, does not want to be saved this way. And foreign-aid experts and diplomats usually just pump more money down the ratholes of already repressive governments. The people of these countries would prefer to save themselves and their families by working in America. After five or ten years here, many will return to their homelands with their savings and job skills.

The best answer to the problems of Somalia and other third-world counties is not to send heavily armed United States troops to save starving children and their parents. Instead, the best solution is to drop our immigration barriers. This would enable thousands of destitute people to nourish their bodies and spirits through labor and life in America. The principle is the same whether the suffering is in Somalia, Bosnia, Croatia, Russia, Ukraine and every other country where political forces continue to limit the freedom and regulate the lives of the citizenry.

For some hundred and fifty years, the United States was the major safety valve of the world. Our parents, grandparents, or great-grandparents came to America to escape the stagnation, wars and famines that were so common under European and Asian despots.

The steady flow of impoverished immigrants to America turned into a flood in the middle and late 1800s. My great-grandfather left Germany in the 1860s, along with over 800,000 other Germans. New rail and shipping lines had lowered transportation costs significantly. And German farmers were having trouble competing with less expensive agricultural goods imported from the new world. So, German farmers had to choose between declining living standards and a long voyage to the new world. Notice, though, that by leaving Germany, German emigrants were making both the old world and the new world better off. Wages tend to rise as people depart since employers offer higher wages to attract replacement workers from the remaining population. In Germany, farm labor became more scarce as the laborers left for the new world.

In America, richer lands were brought into cultivation by newly arrived immigrants from Germany and other nations. And millions of immigrants from the failing farms of the old world were drawn into the booming manufacturing sector, settling in the growing urban centers of America.

But why didn't immigration drive down wages in America? If fewer people in old-world countries tended to drive up wages, you would think that all those people pouring into the new world would drive down wages. Well, yes and no. The American economy of the nineteenth century was dynamic and growing. Immigrants did tend to drive down wage rates for some jobs, but many immigrants took advantage of economic freedom in America to start new businesses, sometimes founding whole industries. Immigrant entrepreneurs vastly stimulated the demand for labor and helped bid up wage rates.

Another of my ancestors fled Ireland, where various policies had so distorted farming and impoverished the people that mass famine followed the failure of the potato crop. Millions died, but millions more escaped to America where they started over. When millions of desperately poor Irish men and women poured into American cities, along with millions of other immigrants, it was like pouring gasoline onto the American economic fire. A rapidly growing U.S. economy spurted ahead even faster.

The analogy is apt. Gasoline explodes when the circumstances are right, and for gasoline the circumstances are right when there is oxygen and a spark. For people, poverty is the oxygen and economic liberty is the spark. The Irish worked hard. Other immigrants did much the same, putting in long days and resting only on the Sabbath. Hard work and frugal habits paid off for most, and they left their children and grandchildren a better life.

Poverty still exacted a heavy toll. Long hours of mind-numbing factory labor paid for food and shelter but exhausted the minds and bodies of city workers, just as manual labor from dawn to sunset exhausted agricultural workers. These were transition years, when machines were slow and dangerous by today's standards. The transition from agriculture to early manufacturing to the advanced manufacturing and service industries of today consumed much of the lives of our ancestors. These hard-working men and women spent their lives creating the wealth many of us take for granted.

So now that the average American is so stunningly wealthy by historical standards (though probably poor by some future standard), it is time to share the wealth—that is, the wealth of opportunity. Even with the massive taxation and economic intervention of our government (which should be ended), our society offers life-saving opportunities for the impoverished millions of the world. And a steady flow of new, industrious people would light new fires of freedom and prosperity not only here but all over the world.

The world benefits from emigration and immigration—economically, politically and culturally—innovation flourishes, wages rise, cultures mingle, and progress continues. The flow of peoples, like the flow of goods, should be free.

Gregory F. Rehmke is director of economics in argumentation at the Free Enterprise Institute in Houston, Texas. This article originally appeared in The Market Liberal, *published by The Knowledge Network Foundation, Seattle, Washington, and was reprinted in the August 1993 issue of* Freedom Daily, *published by The Future of Freedom Foundation.*

20

Clinton, Castro, and Cuba

by Jacob G. Hornberger

August 19, 1994, will go down as a black day in the history of the United States. On that day, President William Jefferson Clinton began jailing Cuban refugees in an American concentration center on the American side of Cuba. It was the first time since the Cuban revolution in 1959 that people in Cuba were freer under Fidel Castro than under an American president.

There ought to be 250 million Americans rising up in anger and outrage over the president's conduct. These Cubans are the tired, poor, huddled masses yearning to breathe free—the people described on the Statue of Liberty. They have suffered for most of their lives under communist tyranny and oppression. They are now threatened with death by starvation.

They only seek to sustain their lives—and the lives of their spouses—and their children—and their parents.

They leave all of their earthly possessions behind. They say good-bye—possibly for the last time—to lifelong friends and relatives. Under cover of darkness, they tie their inner tubes together. They climb into their rickety, leaky rafts. They have little to eat or drink. They see how the scorching sun causes others to hallucinate and jump overboard, into the waiting mouths of sharks. They see arms and legs floating by. They know not what awaits them at the end of their journey.

And still they come.

Where have all the leftists gone?

And what awaits those who make it? Outstretched arms? Joy? Love? Happiness? Freedom?

Not exactly. What awaits them is a penitentiary. A penitentiary in Cuba. A penitentiary organized and run by U.S. government officials on the American side of Cuba.

President Clinton says that it is better that Cubans remain home where they can assist in the overthrow of Fidel Castro.

Now, since when has Bill Clinton become an ardent anticommunist? Twenty years ago, Clinton was asked to give his life to fight communism in Southeast Asia. His response? "Are you crazy? You think my life is going to be sacrificed to stop communism? I'm headed to Oxford."

Today, despite the fact that he was unwilling to give his life in a fight against communism, Clinton says that Cubans should be willing to do so.

And what weapons does Clinton expect the Cubans to use against the machine guns that protect Fidel Castro? Sticks? Sugar canes? Rocks? Unfortunately, Castro and Clinton share the exact same perspective on the issue of gun control: that is, that only the government should own assault rifles, grenades, and other means by which people are able to resist effectively the tyranny of their own government. Hundreds of Cubans would be massacred if they assaulted Castro's machine-gun nests with sticks, sugar canes, and rocks—and it is cruel and irresponsible for Clinton to even suggest the idea.

Clinton says: "The emigration of the Cuban refugees is the result of Castro's failed system." But notice that in speaking about Castro's "failed system," Clinton and others in his administration never go into specifics. What specifically is it about Castro's system that has failed?

Let us scratch beneath the surface and see what we find. As we do so, ask yourself: Does Clinton oppose any part of Castro's failed system? For the last thirty years, Castro's failed system has consisted of:

(1) national health care;
(2) public housing;
(3) public schooling;
(4) public works;
(5) public spending;
(6) high taxation;
(7) welfare;

(8) economic regulations;

(9) guaranteed employment;

(10) trade restrictions;

(11) emigration and immigration controls;

(12) wage and price controls;

(13) antispeculation laws;

(14) government monetary system.

In other words, if we examine carefully the specifics of Castro's failed system, we find—voilá!—the economic philosophy of Bill Clinton! In fact, there is not one aspect of Castro's economic philosophy that Bill Clinton does not wholeheartedly embrace.

And it is somewhat amusing to hear Clinton complaining about the nondemocratic aspects of Castro's regime. After all, when Clinton decided that a 30-year American immigration policy should be changed, did he go to Congress, set forth his arguments, and ask that Congress change the policy? Of course not. Just as his nemesis Fidel Castro does in Cuba, Clinton ruled by decree. Exercising his role as the American ruler, he unilaterally decreed a major change in America's 30-year-old immigration policy toward Cuban refugees.

Where have all the lovers of the poor gone?

No, the problem is not that Clinton has ideological differences with Fidel. On the contrary, their philosophies on the role of government in economic affairs are the same. Clinton and Castro are ideological brothers—comrades-in-arms—they both wholeheartedly endorse the welfare-state, regulated-economy way of life that has brought so much misery and poverty all over the world in the 20th century.

The problem, instead, is a practical one—these ideological brothers had a falling out many years ago. In 1980, Fidel permitted thousands of immigrants to flee to the United States. Many of them were housed in Arkansas, where Clinton was governor. Rioting took place in the Arkansas concentration centers in which the Cubans had been placed. Clinton lost his bid for reelection. And he has never forgiven Fidel Castro for helping to cause his political defeat.

Unfortunately, it is the Cuban people who must pay the price for this dispute between the American ruler and the Cuban ruler.

Of course, this is not the first time that U.S. immigration policy has been used to ensure that people remain under totalitarian tyranny. Recall what happened under the regime of President Franklin D. Roosevelt, who is presented to every child in every public school in America as one of history's greatest humanitarians and lovers of the poor. Unfortunately, those attributes did not manifest themselves in 1938. For this was the year that FDR was asked if U.S. immigration policies could be relaxed in order to permit Jews to emigrate from Hitler's Germany and enter the United States. The great humanitarian's response? "This is not in contemplation. We have the quota system."

One of these days, if Roosevelt and Clinton ever have their faces carved into some mountain in the Rockies, the following words can appear beneath them: "They ensured that people lived and died under Nazism and communism so that America could remain stable and pure."

And what have we heard from American mayors and city-council members about the plight of the Cuban refugees? After all, whenever a local resident opposes a public-housing project in the community, local politicians are the first to exclaim: "You hate the poor. You hate the homeless. You are a racist." One would naturally assume that, with their love for the poor and homeless, these politicians would openly embrace the Cuban refugees. Unfortunately, however, their silence has been deafening. Why? Because they cringe in fear that Clinton will do to them what Gorbachev did to Castro—cut off the millions of dollars in government largess that flows to local politicians and bureaucrats from the nation's capitol.

Where have all the advocates for the homeless gone?

What is Clinton's method of combating Castro's socialism? Clinton (like all of his predecessors) believes that the way you fight socialism is with socialism.

What, in essence, has Castro done to the Cuban people since 1959? He has used the government to control their lives and fortunes—this is the core of the socialist philosophy—that people should not be free to accumulate unlimited amounts of wealth and decide for themselves what to do with that wealth.

And so what does the U.S. government decree? It prohibits the American people from traveling to Cuba and trading with the Cuban people! In other words, to fight Castro's control over the lives and fortunes of the Cuban people, the U.S. government takes control of the lives and fortunes of the American people!

There is only one effective way to fight socialism overseas—with freedom! Americans have the moral right to do whatever they want with their own money—and to travel anywhere in the world without permission of their public officials. It is abhorrent—and a violation of every principle of freedom and every principle in the Declaration of Independence—that an American who travels to

124

Cuba or does business with the Cuban people is jailed by *American* authorities for this conduct.

If Americans were free to travel and trade without political interference, would this mean that Castro would immediately end his socialist system? No. But every time Castro opened the door a little bit—whether by legalizing the use of dollars—or permitting a private hotel to be built in Havana—or selling fine cigars to Americans—American producers and consumers would rush through the opening, without having to concern themselves with interference from American politicians. As private Cubans became prosperous and wealthy, more and more doors would begin to creak open. And the increased levels of private wealth in Cuba would serve as an ever-growing counterweight to Castro's political power. As private citizens flourished, Castro would become increasingly irrelevant.

Thus, it is the United States government's embargo against Cuba that is ensuring the continuation of Castro's omnipotent control over the Cuban people. Even worse, the embargo is causing starvation and death—not for Castro, but for those at the bottom of the economic ladder. The situation is the same as it is in Haiti—Clinton wishes to punish the foreign rulers, and so he imposes an embargo that instead starves and kills those at the bottom.

And it is not simply U.S. government trade embargoes that are causing so much misery, death, and destitution in different parts of the world. America's protectionist policies are doing the exact same thing. When the U.S. government imposes a quota on imported sugar in order to protect American businessmen (welfare for the rich), consider what this does to sugar farmers in the Caribbean, not to mention what it does to American consumers.

Now, imagine the results if the American people required their government to end all quotas, import restrictions, and all other protectionist measures. Economies overseas would begin to flourish as a result of the increase in international trade, especially trade with American consumers! And that increase in prosperity would mean that people would no longer have to leave friends and family to escape starvation and destitution. Emigration and immigration would become a more natural process—one in which people were moving simply in order to find increased opportunities.

Where have all the sixties' protestors gone?

There is one positive aspect of the incarceration of Cuban refugees. At least now the charade behind the welfare state's "We love the poor, the needy, and disadvantaged" is exposed for the lie that it is and always has been. The U.S. government—the government that professes to love those at the bottom of the economic ladder, with its public housing, food stamps, minimum-wage laws, welfare—once again takes off its velvet glove and exposes the ugliness of its iron fist. It slams the door on the Cuban poor and homeless. And then it herds them into American concentration centers far from American shores—on Clinton's side of Cuba, where the hope is that they will ultimately seek asylum in some other country . . . perhaps even in Castro's side of Cuba.

Gone to graveyards every one.

A few years ago, the German people tore down one of the most despicable walls in history. Is it not time that the American people do the same?

When will they ever learn?
When will they ever learn?

This essay appeared in the October 1994 issue of Freedom Daily, *published by The Future of Freedom Foundation.*

21

The Freedom to Move as an International Problem

by Ludwig von Mises

Discussions of the problems of peace and of the League of Nations have made substantial progress in recent months. Today one very often hears that peace cannot be secured simply by decree. Rather, to create a lasting peace, conditions must first be established which make life without war possible. Since it is believed that the "unequal distribution of raw materials" is the primary source of the conflicts that could lead to war, the first thought is for a "more equitable" distribution of raw materials. However, it is not very clear just what this means.

Wool is produced primarily in Australia, cotton in the United States, India and Egypt. Is it now proposed to hand over a part of these territories to the European states who possess no wool or cotton producing areas of their own? Let us assume the most preposterous case, that the wool producing territories of Australia were parceled out among the European states. How would this improve the situation of these European countries? After the new partition, the Europeans would still have to purchase wool, as they did before, from the producers of wool whose lives, after all, are no bed of roses today.

The English also buy wool in Australia. They too must pay for this wool, just as must every other buyer. The fact that the British king is also sovereign over Australia plays no role in these purchases. Australia is completely independent of England, the English Parliament and the

English government—in its constitution, legislation, administration and all its political affairs. English industry is not benefitted, as compared with its continental competition, because a considerable part of the raw materials it fabricates comes from the British Empire. It obtains raw materials in the same way and it pays as much as do German, Italian or Austrian manufacturers. The freight situation for British industry is usually more favorable but this fact would not be altered in anyway by a change of sovereignty. Thus, no one in Europe can say: I am suffering because the state to which I belong does not also include areas that are better suited for the production of raw materials. What Europeans complain about is something else.

There are extensive tracts of land, comparable to those in Europe, which are sparsely settled. The United States of America and the British dominions of Canada, Australia, New Zealand, South Africa and so on, are less heavily populated, in comparison with their nature-endowed potential for production, than are the lands of Europe. As a result, the productivity of labor is higher there than in Europe. Consequently also higher wages are paid there for labor.

Because those lands offer more favorable opportunities for production than Europe does, they have been the goals of would-be European emigrants for more than 300 years. However, the descendants of those earlier emigrants now say: There has been enough migration. We do not want other Europeans to do what our forefathers did when they emigrated to improve their situation. We do not want our wages reduced by a new contingent of workers from the homeland of our fathers. We do not want the migration of workers to continue until it brings about the equalization of the height of wages. Kindly stay in your old homeland, you Europeans, and be satisfied with lower wages.

The oft-referred to "miracle" of the high wages in the United States and Australia may be explained simply by the policy of trying to prevent a new immigration. For decades people have not dared to discuss these things in Europe. Public opinion has been led astray by the smokescreen laid down by Marxist ideology which would have people believe that the union-organized "proletariat of all lands" have the same interests and that only entrepreneurs and capitalists are nationalistic. The hard fact of the matter—namely that the unions in all those countries which have more favorable conditions of production, relatively fewer workers and thus higher wages, seek to prevent an influx of workers from less favored lands—has been passed over in silence. At the same time that the labor unions in the United States of America and the British dominions were constructing immigration laws which prohibited practically all reinforcements, the Marxist pedants were writing their books claiming that the cause of imperialism and war was due to the drive of capitalists for profits and that the proletariat, united in harmony and a solidarity of interests, wanted peace.

No Italian should say that his interests are prejudiced by the fact that the lands from which metals and textile raw materials are extracted do not look to the King of Italy as their ruler. Yet every Italian worker *does* suffer because these areas do not allow the immigration of Italian workers. For this barrier cancels out, or at least weakens, the evening out of the height of wages that accompanies the freedom to move. And the situation that prevails for Italian workers is equally valid also for Germans, Czechs, Hungarians and many others.

One must certainly be careful to avoid accepting the false interpretation that workers in lands where the natural conditions are more favorable for production can fare better by prohibiting immigration than they can if migration were free. If the European workers are prevented from emigrating and thus have to stay at home, this does not mean they will remain idle as a result. They will continue to work in their old homeland under less favorable conditions. And because of the less advantageous conditions of production there, they will be compensated in lower wages. They will then compete on the world market, as well as on the home market of the industry producing under more favorable conditions. These countries may then very likely strike out with tariffs and import embargoes against what they call the "unfair" competition of cheap labor. By doing this, they will be forfeiting the advantages which the higher division of labor brings. They will suffer because production opportunities which are more favorable, i.e., which bring a higher return with the same expenditure than do the production opportunities which must be used in other lands, are not being used in their own countries. If only the most productive resources were exploited everywhere over the earth's surface, and the less productive resources were left unused, their position would be better in the long run too. For then the total yield of the world's production would be greater. And out of this greater overall "pie," a larger portion would come to them.

The attempt to create certain industries artificially in the lands of eastern Europe, under the protection of tariffs and import embargoes, can certainly be considered a failure. Still, if the freedom of migration is not reestablished, the lower wages in those lands will attract capital and entrepreneurial effort. Then, in place of the hot-house industries, artificially fostered by governmental measures and unlivable still in spite of these measures, industries with lower wages and lower living standards for the masses will develop there, industries which will be viable in view of the location. These people will certainly still have just as much cause to complain as before—not over the unequal distribution of raw materials, but over the erection of migration barriers around the lands with more favorable conditions of production. And it may be that one day they will reach the conclusion that only weapons can change this unsatisfactory situation. Thus, we may face a great coalition of the lands of would-be emigrants standing in opposition to the lands that erect barricades to shut out would-be immigrants.

Through its affiliated office for intellectual cooperation the League of Nations is undertaking investigations as to how changes that call for general appeasement may be brought about without war. If these investigations and the conference, at which they will be presented, are concerned only with the problem of raw materials, then their efforts will have been in vain. The major problem will be side-stepped, also, if the proposals are merely for a new apportionment of the African colonies and mandated territories in Asia and Polynesia. The primary difficulties wouldn't be settled either, even if the German Reich were to receive back her old colonies enlarged, even if Italy's share of the African territory were expanded and even if the Czechs and the Hungarians were not forgotten.

What the European emigrants seek is land where Europeans can work under climatic conditions that are tolerable for them and where they can earn more than they can in their homeland, which is overpopulated and less well provided for by nature. Under present circumstances this can be offered only in the New World, in America and Australia. This is not a problem of raw materials. It is not a question as to which state should be given sovereignty over some colonies that are scarcely habitable by European emigrants. This is a problem of the right of immigration into the largest and most productive lands, the climates of which are suitable for white European workers. Without the re-establishment of freedom of migration throughout the world, there can be no lasting peace.

Ludwig von Mises (1881-1973) *was the author of* Human Action, The Theory of Money and Credit, Socialism, *and many other works. This essay appeared in "The Clash of Group Interests and Other Essays" by Ludwig von Mises (New York: The Center for Libertarian Studies, 1978). Reprinted by permission of the Ludwig von Mises Institute, Auburn, Alabama 36849 and Bettina Bien Greaves.*

22

Foreign Policy

by Bettina Bien Greaves

Almost everybody wants peace and prosperity. Certainly government officials profess a desire to promote peaceful cooperation among peoples, and they devote much time and energy to "international relations." Yet almost daily the press, radio, and TV report international tensions—in Southeast Asia, southern Africa, the Middle East, Latin America, or the Orient. As human beings are not perfect, possibilities will always exist for mistakes, misunderstandings, disagreements, and disputes that could grow into widespread conflicts. So the task of those concerned with foreign policy is twofold—(1) to contain local quarrels and (2) to minimize the possibility of such conflicts in the future.

It is natural for people to trade with one another. No doubt men came to understand the advantages of voluntary transactions long before the dawn of written history. Persuading others to part voluntarily with some good or service, by offering them something in exchange, was usually easier than doing battle for it. Certainly it was far less dangerous. Barring force, fraud or human error, both parties to any transaction expect to gain something they value more than what they are giving in exchange. Otherwise they would not trade. This is equally true of trades among friends or strangers, fellow countrymen or foreigners, small enterprises or large—whether located next door to one another or separated by many miles or national borders. Trades may be complex, if intermediate transactions or different national currencies are involved, but the principle remains

131

the same. Both parties expect to gain from a voluntary transaction. So people who trade with one another have both good reason to remain friendly and just cause to resent interferences that hamper or prohibit their trading.

Most consumers care more about the availability, quality, and price of what they buy than they do about who makes it or where it comes from. If a particular gasoline works well in their cars, they don't care whether the oil came from Arabia, Alaska, Venezuela, or Algeria. Consumers will buy Taiwanese shirts, Hong Kong sweaters, Brazilian shoes, German cars, Japanese radios, or any other foreign good, if price and quality suit them. And satisfied customers promote good will.

Economic Nationalism

It is governments, not consumers, that make national boundaries important. It is governments, not consumers, that create national distinctions and promote economic nationalism, often without intending to do so. A tax on U.S. citizens, not required for protecting lives and property or defending the country, increases production costs unnecessarily. Regulations and controls to "protect" consumers, workers, manufacturers, farmers, miners, truckers, the environment, or any other special interest also raise domestic production costs. Benefits to special groups—the unemployed, elderly, handicapped, minority enterprisers, or those awarded lucrative government contracts—must be paid for by others, in taxes or through increases in the quantity of money, which in time hurt everyone. All these programs increase costs and make voluntary transactions more difficult and expensive.

As production costs increase, some producers find their sales dropping so they must curtail production and reduce their work force. Many persons then believe it even more important to enact special legislation, erect trade barriers, or grant government subsidies to support the injured firms and protect them and their workers from foreign competition. But such programs only increase domestic production costs still more. This further hampers the ability of would-be traders to carry out voluntary transactions.

The goal of economic nationalism is to protect domestic producers from foreign competition. Its proponents want to preserve a specific pattern of production. They do not understand the mutuality of trade. They do not realize that both parties gain from a successful voluntary transaction. Nor do they recognize the inevitability of change.

Nothing in this world stands still. People move. The wishes of consumers change. Their knowledge is continually shifting. Changes also take place in stocks of available resources and the most economical places in which to produce particular items. Producers, investors, and workers should be free to move about and adjust to these many changes as best they can.

Any attempt to maintain, for political reasons, some rigid pattern of production is bound to fail. Insofar as production is guided by political, rather than economic, motives, it becomes more expensive and wasteful. When government seeks to reduce dependence on imports and increase national self-sufficiency, consumers must get along with fewer goods and services of lower quality; and their standards of living will decline.

Foreign Policy Repercussions

Restricting imports by government fiat reduces exports also. How can foreigners continue to buy as much from us, if our government restricts their opportunities to earn dollars by selling goods in this country? The mutual gains that come from trading turn traders into friends. But when trading is hindered, ill will has a chance to develop. Frustrated would-be traders look for someone or something to blame. Officials of foreign governments become antagonistic to the U.S. government, for they realize their producers' sales to this country are hampered by our government's interference. However, few U.S. citizens blame their government for imposing trade restrictions. Many even consider the federal government a benefactor. For when imports and exports decline, the federal government often tries to make up for lost trading opportunities by offering those who are hurt direct or indirect assistance—subsidies, relief, new protective regulations, and so on. But such government programs can never compensate would-be traders fully for opportunities forgone, reduced production, and the loss of individual self-respect.

The advocates of free trade pointed out more than a century ago that "if goods do not cross borders, soldiers will." As fewer exchanges take place across national borders, individuals have fewer opportunities to know and respect one another. Antagonism, animosity, and enmity among nationals may arise. We have seen this happen in recent years—in India and Pakistan, Southeast Asia, the Middle East, southern Africa, and elsewhere. Obstacles to the path of trade made transactions across national boundaries more and more difficult, expensive, and infrequent. The common bond which could have turned their international traders into friends was weakened. Those who could have helped each other through voluntary transactions

133

had no cause to come together. They remained strangers and, in time, were even led to consider one another enemies.

Government intervention, which begins by distinguishing between domestic and foreign goods and producers, leads in time to a policy of economic nationalism which actively discriminates in favor of domestic products to the disadvantage of imported goods. This hurts not only foreign producers, whose goods are excluded from the domestic market. It also harms domestic consumers and producers. Production costs rise so that fewer goods can be produced and sold. With fewer goods and services available for everyone, living standards decline.

Localizing Conflicts

The sure way to turn local disputes into widespread conflicts is for outsiders to interfere. The first step in that direction often springs from a sincere sympathy on the part of the strong for the weak, the "rich" for the "poor," the "haves" for the "have nots." Officials of one nation offer to help defend a weaker country against the threats of stronger neighboring states. But by taking sides in this way, neutrality is abandoned. No matter how well-intentioned, such government-to-government economic aid and mutual defense agreements show favoritism which can lead in time to military actions and wars. Through U.S. commitments such as NATO, SEATO, and SALT, as well as various treaties, pacts, and executive agreements—relating to the Middle East, China, Russia, Panama, Japan, various African nations, and more—we could well become embroiled in local violence or border disputes, at almost any instant, almost anywhere in the world.

U. S. involvement in the Middle East undoubtedly began with a sincere sympathy for Jewish refugees who wanted to establish a homeland in Israel. Our involvement in Vietnam has been traced by some to a desire to help relieve France, when she was economically and financially strained by military operations in her colonial Indochinese territories, so as to persuade her to join NATO. "We do not plan our wars; we blunder into them," as history professor Henry Steele Commager has pointed out.

George Washington's advice in his Farewell Address (September 17, 1796) is still sound: ". . . nothing is more essential than that permanent inveterate antipathies against particular nations, and passionate attachments for others should be excluded, and that in place of them just and amicable feelings toward all should be cultivated. . . . The great rule of conduct for us in regard to foreign nations is, in extending our commercial relations, to have with them as little *political* connection as possible." And similarly, Thomas Jefferson urged "peace, commerce, and honest friendship with all nations, entangling alliances with none" (First Inaugural Address, March 4, 1801).

U.S. involvement in this century in two world wars as well as Korea and Vietnam is due to the fact that U.S. foreign policy has been guided by precisely the opposite ideas from those Washington and Jefferson advocated. To contain local violence, a nation should avoid taking the first step toward abandoning neutrality and playing favorites. Thus, we should refuse to add to the many international commitments our country is now duty bound to honor. Then we should move toward the foreign policy recommended by our third President—"peace, commerce, and honest friendship with all nations, entangling alliances with none."

Minimizing Future Conflicts Through Free Trade

To minimize conflicts in the future we should aim to create a world in which people are free to buy what they want, live and work where they choose, and invest and produce where conditions seem most propitious. There should be unlimited freedom for individuals to trade within and across national borders, widespread international division of labor, and worldwide economic interdependence. Would-be traders should encounter no restrictions or barriers to trade, enacted out of a misguided belief in economic nationalism and the supposed advantages of economic self-sufficiency. Friendships among individuals living in different parts of the world would then be reinforced daily through the benefits they reap from buying and selling with one another. Thus a sound basis for peaceful international relations would be encouraged.

Individuals should have the right of national self-determination and even to shift national political boundaries, if they so voted in a plebiscite. For practical and economic reasons, a single administrative unit would be sovereign within the political borders so established. But this administrative unit would have to be responsive to the wishes of the people or face being ousted in the next election. It would have to do its best to protect equally the private property of every inhabitant and to respect the rights of all individuals within its borders, irrespective of race, religion, or language. In such a world, members of racial, religious, or linguistic minorities need have no fear of political oppression for being different. Any nation which adopted these policies at home and in its relations with other nations would help to reduce international tensions and so contribute to minimizing future conflicts. But once it began to play favorites

135

again—to grant privileges to some to the disadvantage of others, to introduce restrictive controls and regulations—it would be re-embarking on the path that leads to friction and conflicts among individuals, groups, and nations.

World Peace

To maintain peace throughout the world, the grounds for conflict should be reduced as much as possible. The first step in this direction must be to respect and protect private property throughout the world. The ideal would also include complete freedom of trade and freedom of movement. Political boundaries would no longer be determined under threat of military conquest or aggressive economic nationalism, but rather by legal plebiscite, i.e., by vote of the individuals concerned. In such a world, the national sovereignty under which one lived and worked would be relatively immaterial.

Daily news reports certainly indicate that we are a long, long way from approaching this ideal. Programs intended to promote world peace often lead in the opposite direction. The various inter-governmental institutions—the United Nations and the several regional political and economic communities—do little or nothing to reject economic nationalism. The debates and proposals of their representatives reveal little understanding of the mutual advantages private traders gain from voluntary transactions. They do not even appear to consider the possibility of leaving trade to private individuals and enterprises to arrange as they see fit. Rather they continue to delegate important powers to various governmental authorities to regulate and control quantities and qualities of imports and/or exports, sometimes even to set minimum or maximum prices at which certain commodities may be traded. In their desire to protect various fields of production within their newly erected borders, they foster economic nationalism over geographical areas larger than a single nation. Thus, although the spokesmen for these multinational organizations sometimes talk of "freer trade," their actions lead to less free trade.

The foreign policy that would minimize future conflicts would promote an economic climate in which voluntary trades among private individuals would flourish because private property was protected worldwide. To create such a climate calls for widespread economic understanding. To maintain it would require eternal vigilance.

Bettina Bien Greaves *is resident scholar at The Foundation for Economic Education (FEE), Irvington-on-Hudson, New York. This article originally appeared in the September 1979 issue of* The Freeman, *published by FEE. Reprinted by permission.*

23

Man's Mobility

by Leonard E. Read

Mobility of goods and services is an elaboration or extension of man's own mobility. It cannot be said that man has mobility except as the manifestations of his labors are free to move. . . .

That the general welfare is served by the free mobility of man's goods and services domestically is generally conceded. Then, why is mobility not equally desirable on the international scale? It is, of course. However, competition—the life of trade—fares badly in international dealings, primarily because arguments against competition can be made to appear more plausible when "foreigners" are involved. . . .

True, many American businesses are less and less able to compete with foreign enterprises, but this is due to costs imposed by overextended government and by the coercive practices of trade unions. It ought to be obvious that the remedy is not in a further restriction of exchange but in removing the practices which are now hampering exchange.

Man's mobility—his own uninhibited travel and the free movement of his goods and services—is the road to health, education, peace, wealth, that is, to human evolution.

Let us exalt, not stifle, man's mobility!

Leonard E. Read *(1898-1983) was the founder of The Foundation for Economic Education (FEE) in Irvington, New York. This is taken from his book* Accent on the Right, *published by FEE in 1968. It was reprinted in the June 1991 issue of* Freedom Daily, *published by The Future of Freedom Foundation.*

About the Authors

Samuel Bostaph is the head of the economics department at the University of Dallas in Irving, Texas.

James Bovard is author of The Fair Trade Fraud, The Farm Fiasco, *and, most recently,* Lost Rights: The Destruction of American Liberty.

W.M. Curtiss (1904-1979) served as executive secretary for The Foundation for Economic Education (FEE) in Irvington, New York.

Richard M. Ebeling is the Ludwig von Mises Professor of Economics at Hillsdale College in Hillsdale, Michigan, and serves as vice president of academic affairs for The Future of Freedom Foundation.

Bettina Bien Greaves is resident scholar at The Foundation for Economic Education (FEE), Irvington-on-Hudson, New York.

Jacob G. Hornberger is founder and president of The Future of Freedom Foundation.

William L. Law is chairman of the board of Cudahy Tanning Company in Cudahy, Wisconsin.

Ludwig von Mises (1881-1973) was the author of Human Action, The Theory of Money and Credit, Socialism, *and many other works.*

Leonard E. Read (1898-1983) was the founder of The Foundation for Economic Education (FEE) in Irvington, New York.

141

Lawrence W. Reed *is president of The Mackinac Center for Public Policy in Midland, Michigan.*

Gregory F. Rehmke *is director of economics in argumentation at the Free Enterprise Institute in Houston, Texas.*

Sheldon Richman *is senior editor at the Cato Institute in Washington, D.C., and the author of* Separating School & State: How to Liberate America's Families, *published by The Future of Freedom Foundation.*

Ron K. Unz, *a Silicon Valley entrepreneur, received more than a third of the vote in his 1994 Republican primary challenge to California Governor Pete Wilson.*

About the Publisher

The Future of Freedom Foundation

Founded in 1989, The Future of Freedom Foundation is a 501(c)(3), tax-exempt, educational foundation that presents an uncompromising moral, philosophical, and economic case for individual freedom, private property, and limited government. FFF aims to influence the course of thinking so that individuals abandon a commitment to the philosophy of socialism, the welfare state, and the managed economy and move toward the philosophy of freedom.

The officers of The Foundation are: Jacob G. Hornberger (Fairfax, Virginia), president, and Richard M. Ebeling (Hillsdale, Michigan), vice president of academic affairs. There are nine members on the Foundation's board of trustees.

Freedom Daily is published monthly by The Foundation. It consists of essays, book reviews, and quotes by freedom's greatest champions. Subscribers come from thirty-five countries. The price for a one-year subscription is $15 ($20 foreign).

The Foundation also shares its ideas on liberty with others through lectures, speeches, seminars, and radio appearances, primarily with Mr. Hornberger and Professor Ebeling.

The Foundation neither solicits nor accepts governmental funds. Operations of The Foundation are financed through subscription revenues as well as donations, which are invited in any amount.

Please write us for additional information. We hope you join us in this important work.

The Future of Freedom Foundation
11350 Random Hills Road, Suite 800
Fairfax, Virginia 22030
(703) 934-6101
Fax (703) 803-1480